Praises for Oaster

Dear Pastors,

Retaining OASTER as our campus development consultant was the best investment we made on a nearly eight million-dollar relocation and construction project for Prairie Lakes Community Church.

Brad helped us to get back on track after making several mistakes while attempting to go it alone. Brad saved us months of time by showing us how to set up planning teams and personally inspired more than 250 members to eagerly join a dozen different teams. Brad's team training was more than excellent; it created a sense of excitement and enthusiasm. He also emphasized the critical need to saturate the entire planning effort with prayer, which was so powerful that it has encouraged us to follow through with an ongoing prayer ministry for the new church.

Brad's unmatched experience with many church development programs offered us a wide choice of ministry, campus, and building concepts. We simply could not have had the efficient, attractive structure that we built without that body of knowledge. Nor would we have our present outdoor amphitheater, which will seat 5,000 people when fully developed. Nor would we have a building and campus development plan that can grow from a 1,000-seat worship center to several thousand in the future by simply adding future phases. Today, we have a state-of-the-art facility with insulated, concrete-formed walls, highly efficient geothermal heating/cooling and ministry wings designed exactly for our emphasis on worship, youth, and small groups.

Brad and Kim also followed up after construction, with many useful ideas for ongoing ministry growth. With OASTER, you get more than a consultant; you tap a wealth of enthusiasm and connect with a great Christian friend.

—Mr. Jerry Carlson
Campus Development Team Chairman
Prairie Lakes Church
Cedar Falls, Iowa

Dear Pastors,

I remember sitting in my office in 2000 wishing there was someone I could call that could help me know what I should do. The church was going well, but we had hit a plateau. Our attendance was approximately 650. We had been up to 900 and then down to 600 and then back up again. We just couldn't break through the 1,000 barrier. We couldn't figure out how to maintain the growth. I would have done anything to find someone who had walked this path before—a person who could act as a coach, a friend, and an advisor.

I had read the books, listened to the CD's, and attended the conferences. These were all helpful. But the thing that made the difference for me were the relationships God brought into my life through Brad Oaster. People who had experience in leading a church through the changes and transitions that I was facing came alongside me and coached me. I will be eternally grateful for their contribution to my life and to our church.

Our church has seen incredible growth and breakthrough since 2000. And with the growth has come much change….

From one location to two locations
Six major building projects
From two to eight services each Sunday
From 0 small groups to over 100 small groups
From 650 people to 2,400 in weekly attendance in four years

We have learned a lot through this process of growth and are continuing to learn more every day.

—Scott Wilson, Pastor
The Oaks Fellowship
Red Oak, Texas

Dear Pastors,

Crossroads Bible Church received such high recommendations from other churches in the Dallas/Ft. Worth area regarding OASTER that we just had to check them out! We are glad we did!

OASTER was a great source of ideas, guidance, and direction. They provided a sanity check along the way as we dreamed of our future and developed our plans. OASTER guided us through the master planning process as well as the design of our first phase. By working together, we developed a great tool for our ministry that fits with who we are as a church and with the community we serve.

—D. S.
Lead Pastor
Crossroads Bible Church
Double Oak, Texas

FUELING
VISION

Hi John,

Thanks for taking the time to
meet with us last week,
I enjoy working with you and
hope to continue our friendship
in the future.

Brad

FUELING VISION

A COMMON PASTOR'S GUIDE TO UNCOMMON SUCCESS

BRADLEY OASTER

TATE PUBLISHING
AND ENTERPRISES, LLC

Published by Tate Publishing & Enterprises, LLC
127 E. Trade Center Terrace | Mustang, Oklahoma 73064 USA
1.888.361.9473 | www.tatepublishing.com

Tate Publishing is committed to excellence in the publishing industry. The company reflects the philosophy established by the founders, based on Psalm 68:11,
"The Lord gave the word and great was the company of those who published it."

Published in the United States of America

ISBN: 978-1-62295-122-2
1. Religion / Christian Church / Growth
2. Religion / Christian Church / Administration
12.11.20

Dedication

This book is dedicated to my Lord and Savior, Jesus Christ, who not only died for me but called me out of the slums of San Angelo, Texas, in 1969, to serve Him full time without sending me to Africa, the Amazon, or some other place where I might have to wear a grass skirt, put a bone through my nose, and eat bugs!

Table of Contents

Introduction

Have you ever been in a situation where people trusted you with their money, dreams, and future and trusted you to make the right decisions? Have you ever been in that situation where the very life or death of your business, ministry, or enterprise hinged on the decisions you made? Have you ever been in that position and had absolutely no idea what to do? That is a miserable situation to be in because you end up being very dependant on the "wisdom" of others to help you make good decisions. Unfortunately, the "others" have no stake in the outcome of your decisions and often guide you into making decisions that best benefit them!

Colleges, universities, and seminaries all train people to be professionals in their chosen fields. Pastors, doctors, architects, and others are very well trained in their specific fields, but few, if any, are properly trained in how to run a *business*. A doctor might be great at diagnosing an illness and prescribing the proper drugs or treatment, but might fail at running a medial practice due to a lack of business knowledge. The same goes for any profession, but even more so if you are a pastor.

I say this because doctors, architects, and other professionals make their own decisions while pastors are usually under the direction of a church elder board. Church boards are very interesting, as sometimes they are filled with very smart business people who know how to run a multimillion-dollar organization/ ministry. Other times, they are filled with people who think they are very smart, but, in reality, have no business running anything.

Then there are the smart business leaders, who, for whatever reason, tend to check their brain at the door when conducting church business. I have seen, otherwise, very smart people make the dumbest decisions when it comes to the business of the church. Many make decisions, or agree to decisions that they would never agree to in their own businesses. It is interesting how people change when they have nothing at stake and nothing to lose.

What are you, the pastor, supposed to do when faced with strategic planning, building programs, or other things necessary to lead and equip a growing ministry when seminary did not teach you how to do them? More often than not, you must rely on the experience, advice, and direction of others. Yet when things go wrong, those "others" magically disappear and you take the hit. Good decisions are the key to developing and maintaining a healthy and growing ministry. No pastor, church board member, or person on your building team will ever spend thirty years developing hundreds of strategic ministry plans or new church facilities for growing ministries all across America. I have. And I want to share my knowledge and experience with you so you can learn from what I have done and not be reliant on outside sources for critical information. Remember, when things go terribly wrong, everyone will be looking at you!

Knowledge is the best tool you can have when leading a business, enterprise, or ministry. As the leader with a stake in the game, you need to be the smartest, most knowledgeable, and, therefore, most powerful person in the room. This book is written to pass on decades of experience and wisdom to you, the one who needs it most. After my first decade of church development, I became very confident in my knowledge, experience, and wisdom. They usually make me the most powerful person in any room when the subject is strategic planning or facility relocation/expansion. It is a great feeling when you know what you are talking about. It is much better than knowing very little and hoping others in the room know what they are talking about because you are betting your career on their advice and direction.

My decision to write this book has come from a multitude of similar stories where church pastors and leaders venture off, totally unprepared, into the unknown and dangerous field of real estate development, only to repeat the same mistakes, some large and some small, but all of which have been made previously by other ministries. Whether you buy the wrong property, build the wrong building, get taken by an architect, or robbed by a builder, far too often, what started out as a pastor's dream turns into a career-ending nightmare. It has been said that experience is a great teacher; only it gives the test before the lesson is taught! This book is the lesson before the test! My hope is that this book will teach you the lessons you will need in order for your ministry to succeed. Caution—the test is coming.

Answering
the Call to Serve

I spent a large portion of my childhood being absolutely terrified of God. I wasn't afraid that God would punish me if I picked my nose or sinned in one way or another. I sinned a lot, and, frankly, the consequences were not too noticeable. C. J. Nelson, my Sunday school teacher, taught me that Jesus already paid for my sins so I figured what the heck, it's paid for anyway. (Cut me some slack here, I was nine years old!) My fear went much deeper than some temporary punishment that might hurt for a while and then be over. I was scared God might call me into full-time service with some type of ministry or missions' organization. Now there is something to worry about!

At nine years old, I accepted Christ in Sunday school at Grace Bible Church in Redwood City, California. Each year I would see a number of missionaries come through our church with their ever-present slide show. The missionaries would show us pictures of the native tribe where God had sent them to tell those natives about Jesus. These missionaries are risking their lives for people they don't even know: people who would rather put the missionaries in a big pot and eat them.

The missionaries all seemed to be super spiritual. You see, my fear was that if I ever became super-spiritual, God would send me into the jungle somewhere, only able to see my family once a year, and spend my time traveling from one church to another begging for money. As a kid, I had no intention of becoming super spiritual. I was going to be a pilot, fly for Pan American Airlines, live in a big house in Hillsborough or Woodside, and drive a cool car. I would keep God happy by sending my super spiritual friends in Africa some money now and then. As a nine-year-old kid, I had this whole Christian thing figured out.

Fast forward forty-two years. What you find is a fifty-one-year-old guy in full-time ministry, serving growing churches throughout America while providing support for a number of Christian ministries around the world. The road I traveled from age nine to today was far from straight. In fact, it was one curve after another, one hilltop summit followed by a valley, then another hilltop followed by a deeper valley. I have owned four real estate development companies; I have been a millionaire twice. I have owned six Ferrari's, two million-dollar homes, a three million-dollar estate, and a couple of airplanes, and I managed to acquire enough debt to make Dave Ramsey choke! Sophie Tucker once said, "I have been rich and I have been poor. Rich is better." I have been what many people would consider to be rich, and I have been what everyone would consider poor. While I agree with Ms. Tucker that rich is better, I would add that there is something far better than rich. I have learned, more than once, that rich can be taken away from you. People have asked me what it feels like to lose a luxurious lifestyle, nice cars, estates, and bundles of money and need to start over again. My answer surprises them and might surprise you as well. The biggest regret does not come from losing equity or possessions; it comes from having spent money on those things in the first place. At one point, my wife Kim and I lost a 3.1 million-dollar, ten thousand square foot home on thirty-five acres, due to circumstances beyond our control. Kim and I moved back to another home we owned. I wasn't sad we had lost the house. My deepest regret was, had we simply stayed in the smaller home we could have put millions into ministries all over the world and nobody could ever take that away from us.

Jim Elliott said, "He is no fool who gives what he cannot keep to gain what he cannot lose." Today, we are better than rich! We operate our business as a full-time ministry, live completely debt free, and invest our resources in that which we cannot lose.

So here I am, at a place I never thought I would be, in full-time ministry serving growing churches throughout America. From 1980 to this day, through my various development companies, I helped several hundred churches to design, build, finance, and pay for functional and affordable facilities that enhance their ministry and equip the church leaders to fulfill their ministry objectives. What most church leaders do once or twice in their lifetime, I have done hundreds of times. This book could not possibly contain all that God has taught me in the last thirty years, but I will share with you as much as I can.

Perhaps answering the call to serve took me a bit longer than most, but I know that I am right were God wants me to be and I am doing what God designed me to do. When you answer the call to serve, you will be rich beyond your wildest dreams.

What Seminary Doesn't Teach You

Wouldn't it be great if there were a book that could fill in the gap between what you learned in seminary and what you need to know in order to succeed in ministry? Perhaps someday, someone will write that book. Until then, this book will fill in many of the missing pieces of what is no doubt a very complicated puzzle.

When I started building churches as a young man in 1980, I never questioned the church leaders as to what they wanted to build or why they were building it. Frankly, being married before I was twenty and with kids coming along at regular intervals, I was glad to have a job. If a church was willing to hire me and pay me to build a new facility for them, then I was thankful for the opportunity and eager to get started. Whether or not this was the right facility at the right time for the church's growing ministry never crossed my mind.

I noticed early on that when meeting with the architects during the design phase, most meetings were with church committee members and I really didn't see the senior pastor very often. Now and then, a pastor would show up when it came time to discuss the worship center layout, but even then, the pastor didn't have a lot to say. I would say that 90 percent or more of the new facility design was left up to the architect and a few committee members, but there were exceptions.

During the mid 1980s, I had the opportunity to work with two dynamic churches, both located in San Jose, California. The leadership that managed these churches did not seem to "play by the rulebook" that defines the title and job description for all the committees you will need when looking to expand facilities. In fact, they had no committees. Not one! The staff knew exactly what type of tool (facility) they needed to reach the lost and develop Christ-like disciples. While most churches delegated the design and construction process to volunteers, these two churches ran the entire process the way a master chef would layout his kitchen. They knew exactly what they wanted, how to lay it out, what to budget for furniture, fixtures, and equipment (FF&E), what ministries and programs the space would be designed to facilitate, and how many times each week the space could be transformed for other purposes. This made my job of managing the design process much easier because there was never any question as to who made the decisions and what they expected from the design team and the end product.

My job, when working with committees of lay members who have no experience whatsoever in designing church facilities, often took on the role of counselor and peacemaker. I have been in more than one design meeting when tempers flared as one committee member cussed out another over different ideas of how a space should be designed. In those cases, the person that was most out of control usually won.

Back in the eighties, it really did not matter much to me if the church turned everything over to committees or if the church staff ran the program. While I got no joy out of pulling all nighters with the stained glass, color selection committee, that was my job, and as long as they paid their bills, everything was good. It wasn't until much later that the difference between the two approaches became apparent to me. As I entered into my second decade of church development, I noticed that I really had two different types of churches I worked for. Now you might think traditional and contemporary, charismatic and not so charismatic, those that pay their bills and those that don't, but that really was not it. The difference seemed to be that some of the pastors treat their position simply as a job. They were seminary trained professionals, part of a large denomination that had been around for hundreds of years, got a nice pay check with additional benefits, answered to some denominational authority, and, for the most part, played it safe. If the denominations rulebook says that this is how you expand facilities, then it is as much a part of the gospel as the Bible itself. Many of these pastors had the goal of putting in their thirty or so years, retire, and move off to "Shady Acres" or some denominational retirement home in Florida and play checkers until they die.

The grand champion of such examples would have to be Ygnacio Valley Presbyterian Church that I designed and built in Walnut Creek, California, in 1985. During the design process, I asked the pastor how many seats he would like to have in the new auditorium. He answered without hesitation, one hundred and seventy five. This is certainly not a church that is going to light the world on fire, but perhaps a nice little neighborhood church. Then I asked the pastor how many adults were in the service last Sunday? His answer, one hundred and seventy five! So I asked him about multiple services and he said he had no intention of going to more than one service. He went on to explain that being the pastor of that church required him to devote all his effort and energy on keeping the sheep that are already in the pen from killing each other, and that adding new sheep was not in his job description! When I asked him what would happen if one lost soul happened to wander into the Sunday service, he answered by saying he would deal with that problem if and when it happens. *Wow*, a lost soul wanders into your church looking for God and you see that as a problem! Now there is a church that doesn't need one hundred and seventy-six seats.

The two dynamic churches in San Jose, California, churches were South Hills Community Church, pastored by Peter Wilkes, and Jubilee Christian Center, pastored by Dick Bernal. While the pastor in Walnut Creek saw his career as just a job to deal with, these pastors saw their position as an awesome responsibility and opportunity to partner with almighty God and play a key role in what God wants to do in San Jose and the Bay Area. Both Peter and Dick took on the role of pastor as a second career, having both worked in the secular world for many years. Peter had been an university professor while Dick was previously an ironworker. When they came into ministry, they brought secular business knowledge and practical experience with them.

What stood out to me was seeing how quickly these two churches were growing. I built a 1,200-seat worship facility for South Hills in 1986 and watched the church quickly go to two services, then three, and eventually added a fourth on Saturday night. I got a front row seat as Kim and I joined the church in 1984. Peter's focus was on reaching the lost and training people to be Christ-like. I had more than one conversation about the need to maintain minimum city landscape requirements, as Peter wanted to tear out landscaping in order to add more parking for visitors (which was greatly needed). I built another facility for them in the early nineties for the children and youth ministries and watched as South Hills completely outgrew their campus. Peter was very intentional about nurturing and training talented young pastors from within the church and many of these pastors went on to start daughter churches in the communities around San Jose.

Like South Hills, Jubilee Christian Center was a disciple-making factory. It seemed as though I could never keep up with the attendance figures as they changed dramatically from one month to the next. I worked with George, Jubilee's business administrator, for months on a particular size worship facility only to see the church outgrow the design before we finished it. Jubilee was leasing buildings in an industrial park on the northern most part of San Jose. Eventually, the decision was made to buy land and build a mega church facility that might contain Jubilee's growth for at least a while.

South Hills Community Church and Jubilee Christian Center were the most successful churches in the San Francisco Bay Area during that time period. Both churches had put in the time and effort to develop long range plans in order to fulfill the calling God had placed on the ministries. God had blessed both ministries with talented and driven pastors who had substantial, previous experience in the secular business world and who were not afraid to incorporate business strategies into ministry applications. Seminaries fail to teach you those busiess strategies, and they are so vital to the future success of your Christian ministries. So what do I know about business strategies and why should you care?

In 1987, I couldn't spell strategic planning, much less lead a church through the process of developing such a plan. I was very impressed with the success and growth I saw at Jubilee and South Hills and knew that other churches would benefit from having a plan like theirs. Fortunately, God had placed me in a neighborhood where most of the people were smarter than me. With the birth of Silicon Valley and the population of successful entrepreneurs exploding, many of my neighbors were adding tennis courts or helicopter pads to their homes. I knew most of them relied on venture capital to start their companies, and to get venture capital you need a business plan. One neighbor, Bill Elder, had started Genus Semi Conductor with only nine dollars and grew it quickly into a multimillion-dollar operation. When the company went public, Bill became a very wealthy guy. I remember he got a Boxer puppy and named the little guy IPO, as in Initial Public Offering, when Genus went public. I told Bill about the churches I worked with and how they should all have business plans if they wanted to be as successful as South Hills and Jubilee. I asked Bill how he went about writing the business plan for Genus Semi Conductor and he told me he had worked with an attorney in

Palo Alto who wrote the plan for him. Later, Bill introduced me to Mario, the attorney, and I learned that he not only wrote Bill's plan for Genus, but also most of the business plans for companies like Cisco, Intel, Silicon Graphics, Atari, and many other Silicon Valley superstars. I was given copies of various business plans and studied those plans to see how the formats might be adapted into ministry plans for churches.

Steve Wozniak, the inventor of the Apple Computer, and I became friends in the early nineties. Steve and I spent a lot of time together taking the fifth grade class from Lexington Elementary School to Apple events all over the western United States. (Once you have taken thirty-five fifth graders to Mac Academy at Caesar's Palace in Las Vegas, you can do pretty much anything!) For several years I had unlimited access to Woz and often asked him questions about how they managed the start up and growth of Apple Computer in the early days. Woz gave me business plans, information on various strategies, and taught me a lot about Apple's philosophy and management style. Woz loves talking about Apple so usually one small question from me resulted in an hour or so discussion. He is without a doubt one of the nicest and most generous people I have even known.

I was shocked at the reaction from a church committee when I went to my next job interview. The room was full of pastors, church elders, and building committee members, most of whom were much older than I and looking to hire someone to lead them through a facility expansion project. I told them about my experience with South Hills and Jubilee and bragged a bit about their successes. Then I plopped down a half dozen business plans from Silicon Valley superstar companies and told everyone that this is where they needed to start. I went on to tell that without a strategic plan for their ministry, they had no business interviewing architects. You could have heard a pin drop! They had already interviewed architects who were all too eager to pull out their paper and start sketching ideas and floor plans. Some architects talked about the need to study existing ministries and develop program documents. However, I was the first, and only, candidate to ask them what they wanted to look like in ten years. I asked them about their purpose statement, vision, mission strategies, core values, short term, mid-term, and long range goals, objectives, strategies, ministry organization charts, primary and secondary targets for outreach, marketing budgets, ministry branding, and more. It was like explaining calculus to a classroom full of first graders. After spending time with Bill Elder and his attorney, and reading dozens of business plans, I was suddenly the wisest person in the room at my next interview. Go figure! At the end of the interview, the church leaders agreed they had a lot of planning to do before considering an architect or design. They tossed everything they had collected from all the previous interviews in the trash and hired me to help develop their business plan. They went on to become the fastest growing church in their denomination.

So why don't all churches make strategic plans? Why don't you start by getting professional help in the development of a long-range, strategic ministry plan? Based on that plan, determine what kind of tool (facility) you need to accomplish your short and mid-term goals. Then develop the facility to accommodate relevant ministries in the areas of outreach, evangelism, recovery, discipleship, and missions. And never put your ministry's future into the hands of a committee/a local architect who have no idea of how effective ministries operate today. You likely don't do it because seminary failed to teach you how.

Certainly the largest and most successful churches have long-range strategic plans, right? Wrong! At one time, I thought it would be valuable for my education to collect strategic plans from the top 100 churches in America, so I came up with a plan: I held a contest and invited 100 of the largest and fastest growing churches in America to send me a copy of their strategic ministry plans. The winner would get a great Callaway driver called the "Biggest Big Bertha." (Goofy name for a golf club, but I didn't name it.) Out of the 100 churches I contacted, only five sent in plans. The best plan I received was from Lon Solomon at McLean Bible Church in the Washington D.C. area. It was not the best I had ever seen, just the best of the five. So I sent Bertha out to Lon. He called and thanked me for the golf club and told me he did not play golf! Some might think my plan failed as I lost a nice driver and did not really gain anything from the five plans that were submitted. I actually did gain some valuable information. Being that only five of the top 100 churches cared to send me a plan and not one was up to business standards, it seemed like there was a huge need for guidance and direction in the field of developing strategic ministry plans for churches.

Many people have told me that when they get to heaven, they would like to hear God say to them, "Well done, my good and faithful servant." I have often pictured what that would be like. Perhaps it looks like some "Billy Graham-type father figure" patting me on the back telling me I did a good job. While that would be nice, I would much rather have Jesus, excited to see me, jumping up and down while screaming, "Yeah, baby, now that's what I'm talking about!" Like when Reggie Jackson touched home plate after hitting three home runs in one game of the World Series, only better! What do I need to do in order to solicit that level of excitement from our Lord when we meet face to face? Maybe there should be a class in seminary where the students have to write a paper on what they would want to accomplish in their life and career that would have Jesus jumping up and down, saying, "Yeah, baby, now that's what I am talking about." Doesn't that just beat spending your career trying to keep sheep from killing one another and seeing lost souls that Christ died for as a "problem"?

The first thing we are going to cover that seminary did not teach you is strategic planning. My goal is to make you the most powerful person in the room when you address your board regarding this topic. Many pastors I have worked with feel intimidated when talking to their elders or committee members about strategic planning because some of those people own businesses. Trust me, just because they own a business does not mean they understand a strategic plan or even have one. I have met a lot of business owners who pastors held in high esteem, only to find out the business owners are genuine knuckleheads. Now, on the other hand, I have had some very smart people on church boards and they have taught me a great deal, challenging my thinking and questioning my tactics. At first, I felt a bit intimidated around those people. But now, I look forward to the opportunity as they help me to improve the process and my services.

The strategic ministry plan is just step one in teaching you what you will need to know to continue to lead your ministry in the direction of its ultimate potential.

Step 1—Strategic Ministry Planning

The first and most important step in a facility expansion process is deciding precisely what you want to accomplish within a predetermined, specific time period, and with your budget limitations. The "Strategic Ministry Plan" (SMP) communicates the purpose of the church, mission of the programs, and helps unite leadership, staff, and church members to a common and defined cause. The SMP is a statement of where you want to be in the future, and how to get there from where you are now. In addition to being the business plan for your ministry, your SMP is a description of a future solution to an existing problem, deficient situation, or vision for the future. Part of the SMP is a Gap Analysis Document, is a comprehensive narrative explanation of your existing situation as contrasted with the ideal or desired future situation for a development plan that is not yet formalized. This needs assessment, along with the overall objective, will define the target for which the facility expansion program is aimed. The needs assessment must define the existing situation, the ideal situation for existing conditions, the ideal condition for future situations (by projecting two-, five-, and ten-year growth patterns), and then prioritize the needs in order of importance.

The most powerful person in the room knows the answers to these questions:

1. What is the purpose, vision, mission, and core values of the ministry?
2. What are the top five objectives we should be focused on right now?
3. What does the organization chart look like for the church we hope to become?
4. What are the inadequacies of our current facility?
5. What options are available as we increase our size and need more space?
6. What will our church look like in two years, five years, and ten years from now?
7. What will our community look like at each interval?
8. How do we prepare for what lies ahead?
9. What are the long-term goals for the ministry?

Step 2—Site Selection

Do you expand at your existing site, or should you consider relocating to a new and/or larger site? Will your current site facilitate your overall objective?

The most powerful person in the room knows the answers to these questions:

1. How much land do we need to accomplish our objectives?
2. How much of our overall budget should be allocated for land acquisition?

3. Where are the nearest utilities located and what will it cost to bring them to the site?
4. What type of off-site improvements will the city require?
5. Will the city require a 'use permit' and can a church facility be developed under the existing zoning?
6. Should the land be annexed into the city before construction, after construction, or not at all?
7. What, if any, environmental issues could hinder the development of this parcel?
8. What on-site improvements such as site walls, parking ratios, building setbacks, and landscaping requirements will be required?
9. What are the fees for sanitary and storm sewer hook-ups?
10. Are water meters in place? Are there separate meters for domestic and irrigation waters?
11. When negotiating the purchase offer, what contingencies should there be?
12. How long should the escrow period be?
13. What are the growth patterns of your town?
14. Is a church site on the proposed land in compliance with the general plan?
15. Will the planning department staff support a church project on the site? Can they stop a church from being developed there?
16. What type of neighborhood response can you anticipate?
17. How much longer will it take for church members to drive to the new site versus the existing site? Is this a deterrent?
18. How much grading will have to occur in order to develop an adequate building site, and at what cost? Will the site balance?
19. Is the land in a flood plain, area of special study, near an active or inactive earthquake fault line, environmentally sensitive, etc.

Step 3—Master Plan

Certain shapes and sizes of building lend themselves to greater beauty and utility on given shapes and sizes of properties. Before a building is planned or a site developed, a master plan should be made. The master plan will show the location of all building units, parking areas, recreational areas, landscaping, and sport facilities. The plan will be developed in a way that takes advantage of the land's finer qualities while strengthening its weaker qualities. A permanent auditorium is usually the most centrally located and most prominent building on the site, even though other buildings may be constructed first. The master plan will indicate traffic flow drainage solutions, automobile entrances and exits, phasing of development, and assures the best use of the property.

The most powerful person in the room knows the answers to these questions:

1. What is a "Master Plan" and why do we need one?
2. How do we maximize the development potential of the property?
3. What is the parking-to-seating ratio required by the city or county?
4. Is the parking ratio adequate for your ministry needs?
5. What is the ground over (landscaping) ratio and how much of the land can buildings occupy?
6. How can the development be phased?
7. What building or buildings should we build first?
8. How do you create ease of circulation between buildings?
9. How do you design the parking layout (remember, first time visitor parking) and keep traffic flow from becoming congested before, after, or between the services?
10. How much parking is actually needed per phase (multipurpose, sanctuary, education, etc.) of development? (You should shoot for a 2:1 or a 2.5:1 ratio at the most.)

Step 4—Architecture

The architect has the following basic duties:

1. To design a functional building that will effectively provide for your church's program needs.
2. To make sure the building is safe and practical, that it meets the building code requirements, and is efficient in operation and maintenance.
3. To design the building to make a proper visual statement and an attractive design contribution to the physical environment and community.
4. To design the facility within the financial capabilities of the church with the best balance of quality, quantity, and cost.
5. To make the design and construction process as smooth and trouble-free as possible.

Architects are like doctors: you have general practitioners and you have specialists. If you have need of a heart transplant, you wouldn't go to a GP. Likewise, you would not go to a heart specialist who was just learning to do transplants. It would be in your best interest to seek out a heart specialist with years and years of experience performing the surgery you require. Church facilities are very unique and require the same expertise of a specialist. As with any profession, architects will experience a "learning curve" as they begin to specialize in one particular type of building. Building programs are the equivalent of major surgery to your ministry. Don't risk your ministry's future by placing it in the hands of an inexperienced architect or even a specialist, unless they can show you numerous past projects that are similar to yours. An inadequate plan prepared by a cut-rate architect is far more costly than the services of the best architect.

The most powerful person in the room knows the answers to these questions:

1. How do you find experienced church architects?
2. Is AIA membership important?
3. How many architects should be interviewed?
4. What type of questions should be asked? What about references?
5. How do you go about rating or keeping score during the interview process?
6. How many interviews with the same architect are appropriate?
7. Can you expect free drawings and ideas before the final selection is made? How do you ask for this?
8. When hiring an architect, how do you know that he will use qualified engineers for mechanical, electrical, and structural engineering?
9. Does the committee have a say in which the architect uses?
10. Exactly what services does the architect provide within his fee?
11. What services are not provided (such as: civil engineering, acoustics and sound, landscaping, etc.)?
12. What will those costs be and who will oversee those designs?
13. What happens if those designs exceed the construction budget?
14. If the design presented by the architect exceeds the budget, should the architect redesign the facility at his/her own cost? Who pays the engineers?
15. What is "Errors and Omissions Insurance" and should the architect be required to carry it for your project?
16. What type of insurance should the structural engineer carry?
17. How long after the project is completed should the design professionals be required to carry the insurance? Is the insurance "Claims Based"?

18. What type of contract should you use when hiring an architect?
19. Can you ask for a contract for schematics only? Design development only? Can you hire someone else for working drawings or construction administration?
20. To what point can changes to the design (floor plan) be made without incurring additional costs?
21. What are "Base Line Documents" and how are they used?
22. Do you need a rendering or a model? What will they cost?

Architectural services are generally broken down into five steps: Master Plan, Schematics, Design Development, Working Drawings, and Construction Administration. You should know what each phase includes, what they cost, whom they involve, and what you get.

Step 5—Capitol Stewardship Program

A Capitol Stewardship Program is an intensive building fund campaign designed to raise money and secure pledges for a set period of time. Obviously, the more cash a church can raise, the less it will have to borrow and pay back.

The most powerful person in the room knows the answers to these questions:

1. What are the proven methods of fundraising?
2. How do you build excitement that translates into pledges?
3. How do you put together a fund-raising banquet?
4. Who are the outside fundraising companies? What do they charge and who is the best?
5. Is fundraising best handled internally or do we need professional help?

6. How much money can our church expect to raise in cash and pledges?
7. What percentage of pledges actually comes in?
8. Can pledges be used as collateral on a loan?
9. How do you keep the congregation involved and motivated during the building process?
10. Is it possible to raise all cash for the building?
11. What types of marketing tools are helpful for fundraising? What do they cost?
12. What types of follow-up help do fundraisers offer, and what do they charge?

Step 6—Working with Government Agencies

Working with government agencies is a lot like having your teeth pulled. I have found that the best thing to do is take several Extra-Strength Tylenol before you meet with them. This will give you a head start on the headache you will have soon afterward.

The most powerful person in the room knows the answers to these questions:

1. When do you first need to meet with the city or county?
2. What department do you meet with first? How do you avoid an EIR?
3. What should be done prior to meeting with the planning department staff?
4. How do you get the planning staff to support your project?
5. What is a negative declaration?
6. How do you prepare a public hearing?
7. Who should represent the church at public hearings?
8. Can a denial by the planning department be appealed?

9. How do you build neighborhood support for the project?
10. Should the church members attend the public hearings?
11. When are the plans submitted to the building department?
12. What is the Plan Check Process? How long does it take, and what does it cost?
13. Know how to work with the Public Works and Engineering Department.
14. Find out what the fire marshal will require and know what the costs will be.
15. You should understand ADA and Title 24 and the effects they have on your building program. If you understand them better than the Plan Checker does, you can save a lot of money or at least get what you want.
16. What will the permit cost and what can be done prior to pulling the permit?
17. Once the permit is issued, when do you have to start work before it expires?

Step 7—Finance Solutions

Non-profit organizations are often difficult to finance. Marketing your church to a prospective lender is not hard if you know what they are looking for and how to go about presenting your ministry. Most lenders have "Rules of Thumb" that they go by when considering a church loan. You need to know what they are and which lending institutions look favorably at church loans. Types of church financing include:

1. California Plan of Church Finance: The church sells bonds to their members to raise finances for construction.
2. Bond companies that sell the church backed bonds to investors outside the church.
3. Building with cash programs using Capitol Stewardship.

4. Denominational Financing.
5. Conventional banks, mortgage companies, and insurance companies.
6. Church Development Fund.
7. Funds from private Christian investors and investment companies.

Once you determine what type of financing is right for your ministry, you need to know the different companies involved in that type of finance. Then you need to know how to interview them and properly negotiate the terms of the loan. Knowing what other churches have previously negotiated will help you greatly.

Step 8—Sound Systems and Acoustics

What good is a building that is completed on schedule and on budget if, once inside, the people cannot hear the pastor or enjoy the worship? Most churches have their in-house "Sound Wizard" who knows it all. The overwhelming majority of churches that let the "Sound Wizard" design their systems are not happy in the long run. Sound systems are not for amateurs. Church sound systems require professional design by people experienced with high quality church systems and sanctuary environments. Acoustics play a major role in design and layout of the sanctuary.

The most powerful person in the room knows the answers to these questions:

1. Who are the top church sound/acoustic designers in the country?
2. Based on your ministry style, what type of system do you need?

3. When should the sound system designer be hired?
4. How do you interview a sound system designer and what do you ask?
5. What does a quality sound system cost? Can it be phased?
6. Does the designer also install the system? What about maintenance?
7. Will the designer train the church sound operator in how to use the system?
8. What type of design accessories might be required (such as sound baffles, sound absorption panels, etc.)?
9. Will the sound designer work well with the architect?

Step 9—Lighting and Multi-Media

House lights, theatrical lighting systems, dimming systems, and mood lighting are important elements when creating an atmosphere for worship and teaching. More and more of today's growing churches are incorporating drama as a way to present biblical principles. Proper theatrical lighting is important in presenting drama and setting the proper mood. To help visitors feel comfortable and welcomed, worship songs are projected onto either overhead projection screens or rear projection screens. Sermon outlines appear and announcements are presented using state-of-the-art computer generated presentation programs. The high-tech church has arrived, and you need to know who to work with in developing proper lighting and in preparation of multi-media presentations. You will want to design for maximum versatility and budget into the cost of the project. As with the sound system, go with the professionals. As technology continues to advance, one company may do your sound, multi-media, and lighting systems.

Step 10—Construction

The construction industry is a very difficult and competitive industry to work with. Many churches are fooled by smooth talking contractors (often disguised as "Church Builders") who know exactly what to say in order to build your confidence and get the job. Many churches have been financially devastated because they failed to "count the cost" and relied too heavily on the builder (All builders know that "Good Church People" would never sue them!). However, the construction process can be a very pleasant and rewarding experience if done properly.

Here are some of the items that you will need to know and understand prior to selecting and contracting with a builder:

1. Know what type of builder is right for you. The different types of builders are:
2. General Building Contractor with a lump sum bid.
3. Design/Build Firm.
4. Project Management Company.
5. Owner/Builder where the church acts as its own contractor.
6. Working with a church member who is a contractor.
7. Church builds with its own forces (volunteers).

You need to know the cost factors, advantages, and risk associated with each type of construction method.

The most powerful man in the room knows the answers to these questions:

- How do you go about selecting a builder?
- Since church structures are unique, how do you know if the builder is qualified?

- How do you interview builders and who gets to bid the project?
- Once the builder is selected, how do you negotiate the contract?
- How do you know that the builder has included everything?
- Should the church require performance and completion bonds? Who pays for them and what do they cost?
- What should an application for progress payment look like? What should it include?
- What is a pre-lien, a conditional lien release, an unconditional lien release, and when are they issued?
- Who should authorize payments to the builder and how do you make sure that he pays the suppliers and sub-contractors?
- Who will check on the quality of work and conformance to the design documents?
- When does the architect and engineer inspect the project? When do the city or county inspectors look at the project?
- How do you handle change orders requested by the builder? The owner? The architect? The city or county? The fire marshal?
- As-built drawings, warranties, punch lists, project scheduling, cash flow projections, and contingency funds must be coordinated and organized. Who does all of this?
- How can the church incorporate volunteer help or donated material to help lower construction costs?

These are some of the major issues that you will face during construction. By handling them professionally and properly, you can save large amounts of frustration and extra expenses.

Step 11—Furnishing Your Facility

Once the world finds out your church is starting a building program, you will be bombarded with mail and literature from every local contractor and supplier wanting to sell you on their service or product. How do you know what pieces of your existing furnishings are worth keeping and what should be trashed? Furnishings not only applies to chairs and carpeting, but to technology as well. From computers and copiers to nursery paging systems and security systems, all need to be included and budgeted in order to navigate through the barrage of literature. Investigating these ahead of time will give you the knowledge to separate quality products from fancy logos and catchphrases.

The most powerful person in the room knows the answers to these questions:

1. Which companies do you believe and who should you buy from?
2. What should you pay for quality furnishings? For chairs?
3. What type of carpet holds up the best in a church environment?
4. Do you use direct glue-down or padded carpet, and where do you use each?
5. What is the best playground equipment to purchase? What does it cost and how about maintenance?
6. Can you buy chairs, carpet, kitchen equipment, cabinets, and other items directly and avoid contractor's mark up?
7. How do you buy kitchen equipment at half price?
8. What type of telephone system is best for your ministry? What does it cost?
9. What type of computer system do we need (servers, operating system, printers, etc.)?
10. Where do you find nursery paging systems?

11. Do you go with a local or national security firm? What other security measures (such as safes) do you need to consider?
12. What do we do with the furnishings and equipment we already have?

Step 12—Working with Volunteers

Utilizing the time and talent of church member volunteers has saved a lot of money on many building projects. Likewise, many churches have spent money having to tear out or replace work done by volunteers because the building department, the architect, or the building committee found the work to be unacceptable. There are many areas of a church's building program where volunteers can be very helpful. A time and talent survey of your congregation will help to determine the amount of help that is available. A volunteer coordinator can then work with the builder to make the most practical use of volunteer labor or material.

Do This: Include the senior pastor in everything. Have a strategic plan for everything. Think about, pray about, and write down exactly what your church needs. Get professional help to develop a strategic ministry plan.

Don't Do That: Go along with what everyone else is saying just because they are the oldest, most prestigious person on the committee. Let the architect have his way, just because he's the architect; think about what your church truly needs.

Goals, Guts and Achieving Greatness: What Does Success Look Like?

Before you start work on your strategic ministry plan, ask yourself, "What does success look like?" This is a question that needs to be addressed from more than one viewpoint. The first is, "What does success look like for me?" Once you answer that, ask yourself, "What does success look like for the ministry?"

Goals

Let's talk about *you* first. When you close your eyes and dream about your preferred future, what do you see? Great marriage, happy kids, growing ministry, secure financial position, debt free, thirty pounds lighter, you can fill in the rest. First thing to do is put these desires in writing and explain why it is you wish to achieve them. Last year I had two main goals. I wanted to get rid of all my remaining debt and lose thirty-five pounds. To shed a little magnitude on those goals, a few years ago my total debt was 2.5 million dollars. This consisted of multiple mortgages, car loans, motorcycle loans, and a time-share condo, artwork, several credit cards, an airplane, and multiple other expenses. And there were those thirty-five extra pounds hanging around.

The key to achieving any goal is motivation. What motivates you to work hard at accomplishing your goals? I was motivated to get out of debt by constantly thinking of what I would rather do with my money other than pay interest and monthly payments on all that stuff. If I did not have to make those payments and either owned everything free and clear or simply got rid of some of those things, I could cut my expenses in half. Furthermore, I could help a lot more people, give more money to missionaries and ministries I support, travel more with Kim, and not worry about the need to generate huge amounts of income just to break even at the end of each month. The task of getting rid of 2.5 million dollars in debt seemed overwhelming, but thinking about the joy of living debt free provided all the motivation I needed! I also tuned in and listened to Dave Ramsey at every opportunity I could. Hearing people call in on Fridays and scream, "We're debt free!" provided additional motivation for both Kim and I. By focusing on the positive, a debt free lifestyle, and not the overwhelming negative, Kim and I were able to pay off the last bill we had and enter into 2012 completely debt free! As much as I tried to imagine and visualize what life without debt would feel like, the reality is even better.

Time and again, people like Napoleon Hill, author of *Think and Grow Rich*, have extolled the virtue of being willing to stick to the path through thick and thin, once you know what the goal is.

Guts

What do you really want your ministry to look like? I am not asking about your board's vision for the church, but rather your personal vision. What will bring you true joy and fulfillment in ministry? Not every church is designed by God to be a mega church and not every pastor is called to pastor a mega church. I have worked with many pastors who feel that their greatest satisfaction would come from serving a neighborhood church of 300 to 500 members. Some pastors told me that while leading a church of 1,200, while the board was looking to grow to 2,000. It is hard to get motivated to grow to 2,000 when in your heart of hearts you want to pastor 500 people. It reminds me of Bill Walsh, a great football coach from the Bay Area. Bill coached Joe Montana and the San Francisco 49ers to one super bowl after another during the late eighties and nineties. After reaching the very top of the game, Bill went back and did what he really enjoyed—coaching college football at Stanford University. There is a guy that knew what he wanted, and even though it meant taking a giant step backward to some, he did it because he knew what he enjoyed.

What is it that you enjoy doing? If it is not being the pastor of the church you now serve, then what is it? Steve Thurman started Fellowship Bible Church in Colorado Springs and grew it to well over 1,000 people. The church purchased a large piece of land just off the freeway and built a new facility. Things were going great. Steve, however, was less than fulfilled. He had always wanted to move to New Zealand and be a pastor to pastors. He gave up what every young pastor dreams of: a successful, large and healthy, growing ministry in one of the most beautiful areas of the country. Steve had the guts to resign from a secure job, follow his heart, and go do what God had wired him to do.

Here is a challenge from me to you. If you are in a position you know is not where you want to be, ask God to give you direction and clarity on what to do. I have personal friends that have served churches for years while asking God daily to get them out of there. But they stayed on because they didn't have the guts to trust God, give up a salaried position, and leave the security of doing a job they despised. In one case, it eventually came down to his job or his family, and, fortunately, he chose his family. My friend quit his job with no idea of where God would take him. But God came through as He always does. My friend now lives in another state, has a job he enjoys, and is much closer to God and his family.

Greatness

The only way you can achieve greatness in ministry is to place yourself right at the center of God's desire for you and operate in the area of your giftedness. When I started out my career as a carpenter for Goodman Church Builders, I thought the construction trades were for uneducated, blue-collar workers who would never go anywhere. I took advantage of every opportunity I had to do something other than church building. When I was twenty-three years old, I bought a cabinet-making company in Morgan Hill, California, and hired my father-in-law to manage the operation. I put a lot of money into the company only to have a dishonest salesman steal everything I had put into it. I lost about $100,000 on the venture and had to lay off my father-in-law. Kim was not impressed. So I went back to building churches.

I have a weakness for Italian sports cars, horses, and airplanes. It would be a lot cheaper if God had blessed me with a passion for stamp collecting or comic books! In 1990, I started and funded the California Exotic Car Club, bought a couple of Ferrari's, a nice trailer and a truck to haul them with, and dove head first into the world of exotic cars. Thanks to Tom Selleck and Magnum P. I., everyone wanted to drive a Ferrari. Unfortunately, after I calculated the cost of the cars, trailer, truck, insurance, maintenance, gas, and advertising, I had to charge people a lot of money to drive my cars. It turns out that while a lot of people like to talk about driving a Ferrari, not too many people can afford to drive one, even if only renting it for the afternoon. So I sold the cars, truck, and trailer and went back and built more churches! Are you starting to see a pattern here?

In the early 1990s, I bought an option to purchase a five-acre property in Morgan Hill, California. I hired a civil engineer to lay out a sixty-five-unit sub-division of single-family homes. I spent six months and a lot of money developing the plans for what was called Llagas Corners. The city of Morgan Hill had adopted a growth restriction ordinance that limited the number of new building permits to 250 per year. This meant stiff competition among developers to get an allocation of building permits. I knew I would be awarded the building permits as the city was in need of low-income housing, and Llagas Corners would provide for that need. The homes I selected were modular homes, built in a factory in Southern California and trucked to the site, placed on a permanent foundation, and have a traditionally-built garage added to the pre-manufactured structure. Eventually, I was awarded the permits I needed to develop Llagas Corners, but I had to split the development over a two-year period. It took so long to get the permits allocated that my option on the land expired. The owner was so impressed with what I was able to do that he refused to extend my option and developed the sub-division himself. While I lost about $100,000 in hard money, he went on to make several million on the development. So I went back and built more churches! Just for kicks, go to Google Earth and type in: Bender Circle, Morgan Hill, California, and you can see my almost first sub-division. In the mid-1990s, I was able to use my experience with Llagas Corners to help Ginger Creek Community Church in Aurora, Illinois, to acquire land and partner with a large development firm to build the church campus, a business park, and a large residential subdivision.

By now you get my point. I was really good at building churches and not so good at everything else. Had I accepted God's calling on my life and focused on developing my talent, I would not have wasted so much time, effort, and money trying to be successful in other ways. Greatness happens when you discover God's unique calling on your life, and you commit to fostering and developing that talent.

Once I accepted God's calling and focused on doing the best job I could at utilizing that gift and talent, there was no limit to what I could do. Four years later, I had the largest church development company in the state of California. Today I work with churches all over the United States and have significant roles in helping to develop some of the most successful churches in the country. And I love doing what I do! I wouldn't trade it for anything.

There was a study done years ago where fifty college students were divided into two groups of twenty-five each. One half were instructed to pursue their passions while the other half went after money. Years later, the two groups were compared, and the findings were surprising. Of the group that followed their passions, twenty had a net worth of more than one million dollars and they were all very satisfied with their careers. Of the group that went after the money, only two had a net worth of over one million dollars and most were dissatisfied with their careers.

Satisfaction in life and ministry comes from identifying your giftedness and passion and having the guts to throw caution to the wind and follow your heart. As we now turn our sights to strategic planning, I would encourage you to use your passion and your heart-felt calling like a tuning fork and make sure your planning resonates with that frequency. To plan otherwise would be a waste of your time, talent, and of God's resources.

Do This: Think about your goals. Write them down. Find what God wants you to do and go after it. Identify what motivates you, what drives you, and trust God to take care of you. Place yourself where God wants you to be.

Don't Do That: Do not let your goals overwhelm you. Don't let your motivation fizzle out. Do not try to keep control yourself. Do not stay in an area of ministry just because it's comfortable!

Why Develop a Strategic Ministry Plan?

Over the years there have been a lot of good books written on the topic of strategic planning. Rather than trying to rewrite those books and come up with another approach or manner in which to develop a plan, I would like to simply share with you the benefits I have found when working with ministries that have a Strategic Ministry Plan versus working with those that do not. Let's take a look at the reasons to have a Strategic Ministry Plan (SMP), and, in being politically correct, the reasons *not* to have a SMP.

Unity Among the Leadership

Years ago I worked with First Assembly of God in Ashbourogh, North Carolina. When the topic of developing a Strategic Ministry Plan came up in a meeting with the elders, they said developing a plan was not necessary as their leadership team had been together for years, and they all knew where the church was going and how best to get there. So I started into my "let's make clear who knows what" list of questions. First, I asked who besides the pastor could quote the church's purpose statement. Not one person! The pastor looked absolutely bewildered, as the purpose statement had been the center point of a three-week sermon series not long before.

Next, I asked each elder to step into the hallway with me. One at a time I asked a couple of questions. For example: will the church ever start a Christian school? The answers ranged from "definitely, yes, and soon" to "over my dead body." The other questions were answered with a similar range of opinions. Following my exercise, I went back into the room and without naming anyone, I read aloud the various answers. (I honestly don't know how this board ever even managed to arrange the meeting!) Their answers were so diverse and opinionated that it reminded me of ten guys in a rowboat, each rowing in their own direction. I was successful in making my point, and, to their credit, by the end of that meeting we had completed the first step toward the development of a SMP.

Strategic Ministry Planning benefit: a united leadership team with everyone moving in the same direction.

Benefit of no SMP: you just go with the loudest person in the room and no one else has to think very much.

Your Strategic Plan Will Be a Tool Used for Evaluating Ministry's Performance

Grace Church is a ministry in the northern suburbs of Minneapolis. At first glance, it appeared to be a healthy and vibrant church. The church is located on eight acres, right off a major freeway, with a 50,000-square foot building that was mortgage free, and an average weekly attendance of around 800 people. What's not to love? With a large staff, a million-dollar, annual operating budget, and no big conflicts to deal with, life was good at Grace. (Until I showed up!)

Inside the foyer was a sign that read, "Grace Church, Where Seekers Become Followers." Sounds great, right? Peter Drucker had two questions he was famous for asking. The first was, "What business are you in?" The second was, "How is business?" Everyone at Grace knew what business they were in—they turn seekers into followers. But no one ever bothered to ask the second question until I did.

To answer the second question, I put together a program analysis team and had them analyze fifty-three different ministries and programs currently running at Grace. After a few months, the team put together a report to present to the church leaders and staff. To start the meeting (this was not my idea), the team showed the elder board a picture of the sign in the foyer—Grace Church, Where Seekers Become Followers. Then, because their presentation was in PowerPoint, they morphed it to read, "Grace Church, Where A Seeker Became A Follower." The team had researched every ministry and every program looking back over a two-year period. The result, they indentified one woman who had accepted Christ as her savior. One!

To drive the point home, the team went on to "count the cost" of running a full-time ministry on eight acres with 50,000 square feet, six full-time pastors, countless volunteers, an annual budget of one million dollars (times two), two Christmas programs, two Easter programs, 104 Sunday services over two years, etc., etc., etc. The end result, one woman accepted Christ as her Savior! So, how's business?

Strategic Ministry Planning benefit: you will have a detailed tool that answers the questions of: "What business are you in?" and "How is business?"

Benefit of no SMP: You will never need to celebrate success as no one will know what success looks like.

Your Completed SMP Will Unite Your Congregation in a Common Cause

South Hills Community Church in San Jose, California, was on a mission to make it impossible for anyone to get to hell from the Bay Area. Anyone from the Bay Area would classify that goal as big, hairy, and audacious! Now a goal without a plan is simply a dream, so they put together a plan. Once the plan was developed, they communicated to the congregation in a way that the church members took ownership of the plan, participated in the plan, funded the plan, and watched in amazement as God directed the church toward the fulfillment of the plan.

Anytime a large group of people gather together and are united by a common cause and purpose, great things can be accomplished. Here are just a couple of examples of recent events brought about by groups of people united in a common cause:

Like Gideon's 300, God can use a few to take down thousands when they are all focused on a common goal. Now let's look at what happens when you succeed in gathering a crowd, but fail to develop or communicate a strategic plan.

While the "Occupy Wall Street" crowds of 2011 succeeded in grabbing the attention of the media for months, spreading the movement from coast to coast, they failed in communicating their intentions. Did they have a strategic plan? Did they have any kind of idea at all? I can't tell. If you research the movement on the Internet, you will find a multitude of stories that tell of the group's intentions, but none of them say the same thing. Once the media attention was gone, the occupy folks and their movement dissolved and they had accomplished nothing for the positive.

Strategic Ministry Planning benefit: There is no limit as to what God can do when He finds a group of people, united together in a common cause and willing to risk it all for God's purpose.

Benefit of no SMP: You will always have plenty of work as you will never attract or retain sharp, intelligent leaders who are accustomed to serving organizations that have clearly defined goals and objectives.

With a Detailed Strategic Ministry Plan, Your Prayers Will Be Deliberate and Focused

Do you believe in the power of prayer? I do! But that wasn't always the case. I cannot tell how many prayers God has graciously answered in my life, but I can tell you one that stands out. Kim and I were married in February of 1980. As a young couple, we were barely getting by on my income, even though I held down three jobs. I spent the early mornings as a short order cook at Coco's restaurant on Blossom Hill Road in San Jose. After serving the early morning breakfast crowd, I headed off to job number two where I grabbed my Kirby vacuum and went door to door hoping someone would buy one. (They would have to really need it because I wasn't a very good salesman.) Then I headed off to cook dinner at Steamers' in Los Gatos. On the bright side, I was always well fed!

One month, rent was due in three days and there was no possible way I could generate enough money fast enough to cover a shortage. For the first time, we would not be able to pay the rent. Two things were going through my mind: first, had I not listened to Kim and kept the tithe money she insisted we give to the church ever since we married, I would have enough to pay the rent. That thought made me angry with both Kim and God. The second thought was since we don't have any food and were going to be homeless anyway, why not drive out to Kim's grandparent's ranch in Chowchilla, California, and spend the weekend there. They fed us well and Grandpa Hart would always fill up our car with gas. The drive seemed longer than usual, and the silence in the car was deafening. I kept my thoughts to myself and kept praying, asking God how he could do this to us. The first night at the ranch went as expected: Grandpa brought out the fatted calf and we ate like kings! I did my best to keep my anger and disappointment hidden. The next morning, Grandpa was up at 4:00 a.m. and going about the business of caring for the cattle. I went out to join him once the sun came up. Kim stayed in the house and helped Grandma with housekeeping chores. Grandma's vacuum started making weird noises, then started smoking and died. Kim went out to our car and retrieved my Kirby demo and continued vacuuming the living room. Grandma Hart was so impressed with the new shiny Kirby that she had Kim's aunt come over to see the impressive machine. While I was out feeding cows and lecturing God, Kim sold two Kirby vacuums! Total commission, substantially more than our rent.

Strategic planning benefit: With clearly defined goals and objectives, you will know what to pray for and recognize answered prayers.

Benefit of no strategic plan: There won't be anything important to pray for so you can spend your time doing other unnecessary thing.

When People Understand Your Plan They Will Support Your Ministry

Church on the Hill is located in McMinnville, Oregon. Senior Pastor Jerry Moen hired me to help him in the development of a strategic ministry plan. I met Jerry through Pastor Bill Wertz, a friend I had worked with at Cornwall Church in Bellingham, Washington, while developing a 50,000-square foot, 1,200-seat, multipurpose building. When space began to get tight at Church on the Hill, Bill told Jerry he should contact me because I specialized in Strategic Ministry Planning and church development. Jerry would have nothing of it! Jerry did not want a church like every other Christian church because he had just returned from Boise, Idaho, where he visited with another Nazarene church that had just finished building a state of the art community center. Their sign read, "The Community Center at Boise First." The facility looked like a community center, not a church. The facility included a café, bookstore, a huge interior play structure called the Kidzone (where birthday parties are held all week long), and a daycare center. Boise First's ministry functioned all week long, just like a community center. Jerry did not want a "church developer," he wanted the guy that developed The Community Center at Boise First. Fortunately for me, I developed The Community Center at Boise First! Once Bill explained the connection to Jerry, I was on a plane to McMinnville.

Jerry and his team were great to work with. We had meeting after meeting of very productive work as we developed and polished what would become the operating manual for the church. Jerry told me that if they never even got to the facility development portion of the work, the strategic ministry plan alone was worth every dollar they had spent.

Following the completion of the SMP, church leadership and staff participated in explaining the SMP to the members as Jerry went to work communicating it to the congregation. He also presented the long-range campus development plan. Once the congregation had a clear understanding of the who, what, where, when, and why of the ministry, Jerry introduced phase one of the facility expansion program.

As a result of taking time to develop a strategic ministry plan, a long-range campus development plan, and utilizing a well-planned communications effort, Jerry and the leadership at Church on the Hill had no problem raising the funds to expand their facilities and overhaul their existing building. Jerry told me the biggest benefit was having all staff, elders, and ministry leaders on the same page.

Benefit of Strategic Ministry Plan: As Paul put it in 1 Corinthians 1:10: *"Be of one mind, united in thought and purpose."* When your congregation and members understand and support your strategic plan and campus development plans, you will have no problem funding your vision. People support plans they clearly understand.

Benefit of no Strategic Ministry Plan: Without a plan, or even a clue, it won't take long to count your offerings. People will invest their money with other ministries who know what they are doing.

So, why develop a strategic plan? A successful Strategic Ministry Plan will:

- Lead to action
- Build a shared vision based on common values
- Be an inclusive, participatory process in which church leadership takes on shared ownership
- Leads to accountability
- Be based on useful, quality data
- Require an openness to question the status quo
- Be a key part of effective management

Do This: Develop a Strategic Ministry Plan. Create a team that is united, keeping everyone on the same track. Create a detailed tool to answer all the questions. Trust God to break boundaries and defy the limits. Know what to specifically pray for. Explain the plan to the congregation in a way they understand.

Don't Do That: Go with the loudest person in the room. Work in circles, never seeing success. Fear change and never give the trust over to God. Do unnecessary things that have no effect on what you're working toward. Keep your congregation in the dark in regard to your plan.

A Flight Plan for Your Ministry

Have you ever tried to piece together a model without any directions? Or maybe you had directions, but just didn't bother to read them! My experience has always been that if you're assembling something or trying to achieve something, a set of directions is very useful. Whenever I try to accomplish a goal, or if I want to complete a complicated task, I first look to see if there is a set of directions I can get my hands on. Steve Jobs, when designing Apple products like the iPhone, wanted the phone to be so user friendly so that it did not require a manual to use. Because of this, the directions that come with an iPhone are minimal at best. Then someone came along with a book and titled it, *The Book That Should Have Come with Your iPhone,* and that book sold millions of copies! For some people, the use of an iPhone is intuitive, and for others, well, we buy the book!

Bad Flight Instructors

I fired my first flight instructor because he was not a very good instructor. His name was Ken and I referred to him as "Pilot Ken." While Pilot Ken was a nice guy, he had no step-by-step strategy to teach me the various maneuvers. One day we would practice "slow flight," then "S" turns followed the next lesson by power on and power off stalls. After several days of those maneuvers, a couple of days of "touch and go's," and then back to slow flight again. Now I am all for mastering a maneuver, and there is nothing better than practice to get it right. Once I have got it, however, I don't like going back just for the sake of filling up Pilot Ken's logbook and wallet! This started to get on my nerves. A student pilot should be able to solo and get their license with around fifty hours of actual flying time. While I may not be the sharpest knife in the drawer, I saw no reason that I should have 100 hours in my logbook and Pilot Ken still wanting me to go practice with him, and my not having soloed yet!

As it turned out, Pilot Ken did this with most of his students. If you think about it, why would he train his students and have them get their license in fifty hours when he could stretch it into 100 hours and log the time in his book? Not to mention, getting paid for it. Eventually, I fired Pilot Ken and hired Mike Hogan. Mike is one of those, "been there, done that" former military pilots who had seen it all. Twenty years my senior, he simply enjoyed flying. Teaching students to fly was a great way to spend his retirement time while earning extra money. Mike taught me more in the first lesson than Pilot Ken had in the previous fifty hours. When Kim decided she wanted to get her pilot license, Mike set out a detailed set of directions, checked them off as Kim mastered the various maneuvers, and she got her license in half the time it took me. When I went back to flying school to get my instrument rating, I looked for a school with a very detailed, step-by-step course that showed me exactly what needed to be learned and mastered in order for me to qualify for and pass my instrument check ride. Today, in the United States, the percentage of people who start flying lessons but never finish by actually getting a pilot's license is 80 percent! If flight schools would like to graduate more than 20 percent of their students, they should develop a program that identifies exactly what the students need to learn, give them a step-by-step program to master those maneuvers, and show them with each flight that they are one step closer to the achievement of their goal. A lot more people would accomplish their goals of being pilots.

Spiritual Holding Patterns

Many pastors and churches I meet are just like Pilot Ken. While I have never met anyone who went to church hoping to become a pilot, I do know people who go to church hoping to get their lives straightened out. Unfortunately, while many churches want to reach the lost and develop Christ-like disciples, they have no detailed game plan describing how to do it. They may have programs for evangelism and discipleship, but they do not have a detailed set of instructions defining a road map to spiritual maturity.

Just like student pilots who go to the airport every week, hoping to someday become a pilot, Christians all over America go to church week after week after week, year after year, hoping to grow closer to God and learn to follow Jesus. Yet they fail. Why is that? I believe it is because most churches do not have a step-by-step strategy for developing Christ-like disciples. People go to church for years or even decades and are stuck in a spiritual holding pattern, going around and around until, just like me with Pilot Ken, they have had enough. They leave the church.

If your church is in the business of developing "fully devoted Christ followers," do you have a step-by-step plan? Is it communicated in a way that your members can use it and monitor their progress? Are they being encouraged to move through the plan? And can they tell if they are closer to achieving their goal today than they were last year? I have worked with a lot of churches over the years and I can count on one hand the number of churches, regardless of size, that actually had a strategy for determining where a person is spiritually, where they need to be, and had a plan for moving them in that direction.

Successful flight schools have very detailed curriculum. Every step required to get your pilot license is spelled out in detail. As you accomplish a step, you check it off and go on to the next step. Progress might seem slow at first, but it doesn't take long before you look back and see how far you have come. There is nothing more encouraging than knowing you are much closer today to the achievement of your goal than you were just a short time ago. Take the time to devlop a strategy for moving people in your church from once a month attenders to knowing God personally and getting their lives patched up, then they will be ready to be discipled and go out and make disciples!

Creating Your Flight Plan for Success

If your church is going to be listed among the 100 fastest growing churches in America, you better have a plan! Many churches say they exist to turn irreligious people into fully devoted Christ followers, but they have no detailed plan on how to accomplish that purpose. I frequently visit churches that have thousands of people attending, two or three times per month, who enjoy a good service with great worship and a relevant message, only to return home to a fairly screwed up life. Church should be about life change, not putting on a good show. If people are not actively growing in their spiritual walk and becoming more and more Christ-like, then the church is not doing its job.

When Kim and I fly our Cirrus across the country, we first file a flight plan. Let's say we are going to fly from San Francisco to Raleigh, North Carolina. That is a pretty good trip, so we will break up our flight plan into four smaller legs. We will divide the 2,400-mile trip into four legs of 600 miles; each will take three hours to complete. So now our trip starts with a flight from San Francisco to Richfield, Utah, then the second leg, which will take us to Oakley Municipal Airport in central Kansas. From Oakley, we will go to St. Louis and then take the final leg to Raleigh. At each stop we can rest up, stretch our legs, grab a bite to eat, check the weather, confirm our route to the next stop, make any needed adjustments, and continue on our way.

As a student at the Palo Alto Military Academy, it was a long way from Buck Private to Senior Captain. Fortunately, that journey was broken up into multiple stages consisting of PFC, Corporal, Sergeant, Master Sergeant, Lieutenant, Second Lieutenant, Captain, and Senior Captain. At every step in my journey from Private to Senior Captain, I was given recognition, responsibility, and another stripe or bar on my uniform. For most of my time at the Academy, the rank of Senior Captain seemed out of reach, but the next step was always obtainable. Once I was promoted to Second Lieutenant, Senior Captain was suddenly within reach.

When I was working my way up in the horse show circuit with Beaver (my horse and best friend), there were awards and recognition at each step of the journey. From no ribbon at all (embarrassing), to yellow, red, and eventually blue ribbons, then silver platters, and then belt buckles the size of trashcan lids, every accomplishment was recognized and rewarded. There is a great deal of satisfaction that comes when you know you are moving closer and closer to the fulfillment of a life-long goal. The journey toward spiritual maturity is no different.

When was the last time that you, as a church leader, recognized someone for their achievement in spiritual development? Just think of the thing people accomplish while on their journey to spiritual maturity. The steps might look like this:

- Visited your church at the invitation of a friend
- Accepted Christ as their Savior
- Completed Christianity 101 class

- Became a member
- Was baptized
- Joined a small group
- Began tithing
- Became a mentor
- Led a small group
- Went on a mission trip
- Invests into the lives of others, inviting them to experience the journey

What would it be like if you and your leadership team came alongside people and encouraged them, coaching them through their spiritual development process? From thanking a guest for taking the time to visit your church, to congratulating the church leader who invited them, encouragement and acknowledgement of one's growth is all it takes to motivate someone on to the next step! You can only do this if you have a well thought "flight plan" that, like a good set of blue prints, will show a step-by-step path toward spiritual maturity.

Turn Spiritual Growth into a Great Adventure

Many of the churches I have worked with around the country have developed themes for their spiritual growth plans. At Yosemite Church in Merced, California, the church leadership developed a strategy where church members would travel through Yosemite National Park and work their way to becoming a master climber and guide. When a person joined the church, they were issued a "park pass," giving them unlimited access to the park; when they were baptized, they receive a mountain climbing certificate. They climb Half Dome by completing the spiritual growth class, and they conquer El Capitan by completing other classes. Before long, they are a master climber and helping others to check waypoints on their "park pass."

In rural Georgia, we helped Grace Church design a NASCAR theme to their spiritual growth plan. People start out in the "Pit Crew" until they earn their "Rookie Drivers" certificate. Before long, they are on the track and advancing through the gears as their spiritual growth accelerates. Next, they can earn NASCAR points as they conquer Atlanta Motor Speedway by completing their Financial Peace course. When you commit to tithing, you get a much faster car! Soon, you are giving "pit crew" members rides in your car and helping them get their rookie license. Now and then, you make a pit stop and fuel up, change your tires, and prepare for the next race.

There is no limit to what you can do to make the journey of spiritual development a great adventure. But wait! Please do me a favor. If your church is located at 7,000-foot elevation, high in the Rocky Mountains and a hundred miles from any body of water, don't do the sailing thing! Go climb a mountain, ride the rapids, or come up with a fishing theme! Be relevant and authentic in all you do.

The Smartest Person in the Room

If churches are about life transformation, they need a plan. Preaching great sermons, having great music, and drawing large crowds on weekends while failing to develop fully devoted Christ followers is not what God had in mind. For most people today, God is nothing more than a weekend hobby. You and your leadership team need to develop a proactive game plan that will encourage and motivate people to take a step-by-step journey toward spiritual maturity. These steps need to have a profound impact on the people who commit to and complete each step. I will guide you through a step-by-step process to develop your plan in the next three chapters.

Do This: Develop a detailed, step-by-step plan for spiritual development. Market that plan to your people by highlighting the benefits that come with spiritual maturity. Recognize and reward those who take the leap and commit to a life-long process of learning. Make it fun, interesting, and rewarding by creating a theme that encourages participation. If you do this as a church, you will never lack for volunteers and leaders in your church.

Don't Do That: Do not rely on people to get involved with their own spiritual development without a plan, encouragement, guidance, and motivation from the church. For some reason, here in America, it has become acceptable that 20 percent of a congregation carries 80 percent of the load. That is true for those who serve, those who carry the financial burden, and for those who pursue Christ likeness. That means that 80 percent are riding on the efforts of the 20 percent, and for some reason that is acceptable. When I went to school, anything less than 79 percent was an "F"! Why should we ever think that 20 percent is good enough for God?

Strategic Ministry Planning

My goal is to share with you what works based on my experience. Now, if you are wondering, "How does Brad know what works?" let me fill you in. Many of the churches I have worked with in the development of Strategic Ministry Planning have been listed in Outreach Magazine's list of the "100 Largest & Fastest Growing Churches in America." These churches were small when I first worked with them and today represent some of the largest and most successful churches in the country. While I give God the credit for every church's success, I also thank Him for allowing me to participate in the process.

Let's start with the elements of a Strategic Ministry Plan. First, we will break the plan into two parts. Part one is the Strategic Plan. Part two is the Tactical Plan. While the Strategic portion answers the questions of who, what, where, when, and why, the Tactical part focuses on the implementation and the "how" of the plan.

The word strategic comes from the word strategy, which can be defined as "Determining direction, control, and focus of actions and resources."

The components of a Strategic Ministry Plan can be defined as:

Part One—Strategic Plan

- Purpose—The reason you exist as a church
- Vision—A picture of the preferred future
- Mission—An action is response to purpose in pursuit of vision
- Core Values—Values that govern the operation of the church.
- Goals—Specific and time based accomplishments to be achieved by implementing strategies in pursuit of ministry objectives.

Part Two—Tactical Plan

- Ministry Action Plan (MAP)—The MAP will identify the who, what, where, when and how for each ministry area.

Purpose

This statement identifies a ministry's fundamental reason for existence. A good example of a proper purpose statement from the United States Military might read: *Our military exists to defend the people, property, and interest of the United States of America both at home and abroad.* That statement will not change. It is the same today as it was years ago.

Most churches, but not all, base their purpose statement on the Great Commission from Matthew 28. A typical purpose statement might reference reaching the lost and building Christ-like disciples. While it is not up to me to tell you what your purpose statement should be, allow me to point you in the general direction. First off, keep it simple. If you were to start up a conversation with a non-Christian, could you tell them why your church exists by quoting your purpose statement? More importantly, could that person then repeat it back in their own words why your church exists?

The idea is to keep it simple. Do not write some long, drawn-out statement written in "Christianese" or code that is designed only for those in the know or to impress some seminary professor. Your purpose statement should not require an explanation to understand it.

Example:

"*Crossroads is an embracing community of Christ followers committed to encouraging people to experience a life-changing love relationship with God!*"

I like this because it clearly states who they are: embracing community of Christ followers, followed by what they do, and what they encourage people to do. Furthermore, this statement can be defended as it is backed up by biblical teaching: the most important command—Matthew 22:34-40.

Crossroads is also committed to encouraging people…

> …to experience a Christ-like love for each other, based on the New Command—John 13:34-45

> …to experience a compassionate love for the lost, based on the Last Command—Matthew 28:18-20

Vision

What would you like your future to look like? There is a saying, "If you don't know where you are going, then you will likely end up somewhere else." Let's face it, we are all going somewhere, so why not predetermine where you want to go and come up with a proactive plan that moves you in that direction?

When Disney World in Florida opened for the first day, Walt Disney was not there. He had died before the park was finished. Many people felt bad that Walt did not live to see his dream completed, although that is not how Walt saw it. He was able to accomplish great things during his life because he had learned to *work backward!* Walt always started with a completed vision. He could describe Disney World in great detail before he ever purchased the property in Florida. What started out as a dream made its way to sketches, then detailed plans, and eventually it became reality. Without the dream, there would be no plan, and without a plan, there would be no Disney World. Walt Disney did not have to see Disney World finished in order to experience it.

One of my favorite examples of what a person can accomplish with a vision and a commitment to the fulfillment of that vision is the extraordinary life of Arnold Schwarzenegger. While there are no rewards in heaven for becoming a seven-time Mr. Olympia, a Hollywood actor with forty-three movies, husband of a Kennedy, and the governor of California, Arnold's accomplishments demonstrate what a person can do in this country once they commit to it. What differentiated Arnold from his brother was that Arnold had a dream and a commitment to seeing it to fruition.

So what is your dream? What would you like to put at the foot of the cross when all is said and done, as evidence of a life well lived serving God? If Walt Disney and Arnold Schwarzenegger can accomplish what they did, what can God do through you? The only limiting factor is you. Maybe what God wants to accomplish through you is to have a small neighborhood church where a loving and caring pastor can genuinely care for 300 people and know each person by name. Or maybe you will start a dozen churches. Are you willing to go with God?

Now, envision what your church will look like ten years from today if all growth barriers were removed and the church was free to pursue its ultimate potential.

In describing that picture, make it SMART!

S = Strategic
M = Measurable
A = Attainable
R = Realistic
T = Time bound

Example: By the year 2025, our church will be a healthy, growing church of 2,000 or more, meeting on our fully developed campus with multiple venues and planting a daughter church every five years.

You can now see where you want to be and when you want to be there. The next step is to work backward from that determined destination and build a plan to get you there.

Mission Statement

Over the years, I have seen many churches confuse their purpose statement with their mission statement. Many people have said, and authors have written, that it really doesn't matter if you call your statement a purpose statement or a mission statement. Let me bring some clarification to this topic. It is critical to the success of your ministry to understand the difference between your purpose and your mission. While your purpose statement describes why your ministry exists, your mission statement tells how your ministry goes about accomplishing your purpose. Your purpose statement should never change, and your mission statement must change on a regular basis in order to keep up with changing environments both inside and outside the church.

Back to our military example. The United States military exists to defend the people, property, and interests of the United States of America both at home and abroad. The statement answers the "why" regarding our need for military and armed forces. The mission statement will address the "how." During the period of the last two hundred years, the "how" has changed many times. During this time period, our military has fought two world wars, a war in Korea, Vietnam, Iraq, and Afghanistan. Each of those conflicts represents a mission where our military was deployed in defense of the purpose statement.

With your purpose statement written, you clearly know why you exist. Your completed vision statement clarifies where you are going. Now let's work on how your will get there. To do that, let's work with the following purpose statement: "Our church exists to turn un-churched people into fully devoted followers of Christ."

Step 1—If you are going to turn un-churched people into anything, you must first come into contact with un-churched people.

Step 2—Once you have contact with the un-churched, you must introduce them to Christ in a compelling manner.

Step 3—There are no perfect people, so you must address people's broken lives and help them to live full and productive lives.

Step 4—God has uniquely wired people with spiritual gifts that they can discover and develop in order to serve Him. This step will give people the opportunity to discover, hone, and polish those gifts in preparation for a life of service to God.

Step 5—The church should provide opportunities for people to use their gifts in furthering the purpose, mission, and vision of the ministry of the body of Christ.

Our five-step mission strategy provides you with an outline identifying the steps necessary to fulfill your purpose as you move closer to the fulfillment of your vision. The mission strategy needs to be communicated in a way that your congregation will both understand and remember it. For example, you might wish to communicate the five steps above as follows:

Catch 'em—Catch lost people because they matter to God
Hatch 'em—Hatch them into a relationship with Christ
Patch 'em—Patch their broken lives

Match 'em—Match them with their spiritual gifts
Dispatch 'em—Dispatch them back into the world to catch
more lost people

South Hills Community Church				
SHCC exists to turn the unchurched in our community into fully devoted followers of Christ				
Catch'em	**Hatch'em**	**Patch'em**	**Match'em**	**Dispatch'em**
Catch'em ministries exist because lost people matter to God.	Hatch'em ministries exist to guide people into a new relationship with Christ.	Patch'em ministries exist to assist people in the restoration of broken lives.	Match'em ministries exist to connect people with their spiritual gifts.	Dispatch'em ministries exist send people into the world to catch more lost people.
Target Non Christian	Target Baby Christian	Target Growing Christian	Target Maturing Christian	Target Christian Leader
Community Outreach Programs	Christianity 101 Classes	Christianity 201 Classes	Christianity 301 Classes	Christianity 401 Classes
Outreach ministries and programs are designed to connect SHCC with those in our target area who do not yet know Christ or SHCC.	Discovering Christ is a 4-week seminar that helps you to understand the Christian faith and what it means to be a Christ Follower.	Establishing a Life of Faith is a one-session seminar that marks your growth and increased commitment.	Becoming a Minister of Christ is a one-session seminar that serves as the checkpoint at the start of the third stage. Topics that are covered in this seminar include spiritual gifts, lay ministry, and the purpose of the church.	The 401 Interview is an opportunity to individually recognize and celebrate your spiritual growth. This personal conversation with the senior pastor is simply a time to learn more about your unique spiritual experience and future as a role model in the church body.
Outreach events include: MOP's Wilderness Ministries South Hills Riders Celebrate Recovery R-Groups Hope for the Separated People helping People Point Man Ministries Admit One Business Network Meals Ministry Building Trades Ministry	Beginning to grow in God's family is an 8-week class designed to help you get integrated into the church body and begin to live the Christian life. Introduction to the Bible is a 12-week class that answers some basic questions about the Bible and helps you become a lifelong student of God's word.	The 2-7 Series is a series of three 12-week studies that helps you develop spiritual habits and a Christian perspective. Topics include prayer, Bible study, Scripture memory, Christian living, and witnessing. The three classes that form this series are: Growing Strong in God's Family, Deepening your Roots in God's Family and Bearing Fruit in God's Family. Overview of the Bible is a 12-week class covering the "big Picture" of the Bible.	Answering God's call to ministry is a 12-session class that helps you discover your gifts and develop your personal ministry. Theology of the Gospel is a 12-session class that explores in depth the core doctrines of the Gospel of Christ.	"Consumed with Christ" Retreats are yearly weekend retreats designed to provide you an opportunity to renew your commitment, reflect on your spiritual life, and be challenged by others to continue your pursuit of Christ-likeness.
To maintain our growth goal of 20%, we must engage 2000 people in a "meaningful connection" with SHCC each year and encourage them to take the next step.				
2000 Meaningful Connections	500 New Converts	300 Adult Ed. & Small Groups	150 Missions Trips	50 Leadership Training

In working with churches toward the development of their mission strategy, I have seen as little as three steps and as many as seven steps. To go beyond seven is to move into the tactical part of the strategic plan and risk the chance that people will not remember them.

Other examples of effective mission strategies include:

Connect, Win, Grow, Equip, Send
Explore, Embrace, Encourage, Engage and Empower
Reach, Relate, Restore, Teach, and Release

A church in Norther Minnesota came up with this one:

Bait 'em, Hook 'em, Net 'em, Clean 'em, and Fry 'em. Personally, I saw nothing wrong with it, but the elders felt it lacked that "seeker friendly" feel they were after!

Core Values

Core values are a set of internal values that govern your ministry and will guide behaivors and relationships within the church—both internally and externally. You will usually have five to seven core values. Having more than seven dilutes the value of what you are claiming.

The first time I ever saw Bill Hybels at Willow Creek Community Church was in the early nineties. I was working with Tom Greer and the Design Team from Saddleback Church. During our tour of Willow Creek, we were standing in the atrium area having a conversation. I noticed Bill walking along an upper hallway that was open to the atrium. He suddenly stopped in front of a classroom and ripped down a sign that had been taped up onto the door. He mumbled something and stormed off. I later learned that one of the core values at Willow Creek is excellence, and excellence honors God and inspires people. Apparently, the handwritten sign Bill removed did not meet the standard of excellence.

While visiting a church in Florida, I noticed their children's playground was made up of old railroad ties, carelessly nailed together to make some type of climbing structure. This structure looked like a health hazard and a potential lawsuit waiting to happen. Later, I found "excellence in children's ministry" on their list of core values! I told the church leadership that excellence in children's ministry was not a core value because their hokey play structure was far from excellent. They either needed to remove that core value and stick to the truth, or demonstrate the value by replacing the play structure.

Don't lie when putting together your core values! (One of my own core values is "Tell It Like It Is." I am not sure my publisher will like that when this book is edited, but for now, I will tell it like it is.) Lying on your list of core values is pretending to be someone or something you are not. Be honest and genuine while undertaking this self-evaluation.

Try to keep your list to seven or less. Churches that have thirty core values actually have no core values at all. Be very deliberate with the words you choose to use. Then, next to the core value, give a brief definition of what the core value means.

Here is an example of what I would look for in a completed list:

- Relationships—We believe quality relationships allow extraordinary things to happen!
- Encouragement—We know an encouraging community is essential in helping people live for God.
- Authenticity—We promote authenticity by being open and honest with God, ourselves, and each other.
- Leadership—We honor those in leadership because they are accountable to God.
- Excellence—We offer God our best in all we do!
- Relevance—We commit to being relevant by using ever-changing methods to communicate the never-changing message.

Core values need to be expressed in everything your ministry does. If a program is being conducted, whether by staff or volunteers, and fails to demonstrate your core values, that leader needs to be confronted and reminded of the core values. A grumpy flight attendant might be tolerated on most airlines, but not on Southwest Airlines. A grumpy flight attendant would first be confronted by other flight attendants. If that did not work, he or she would be sent to the director's office! For your ministry to succeed, it must operate within a defined set of core values. Those values must be clear, concise, and obvious to everyone.

Goals

Goals are general guidelines explaining what you intend to achieve in your ministry. There are short-term, mid-range, and long-term goals. At this point in the Strategic Ministry Plan, keep your goals fairly general. In the second half of the SMP, the tactical portion, we will identify goals for each ministry department.

Goals should be:

- Measurable (or they are only good intentions)
- Realistic (or they will set your ministry up for failure)
- Rewarded when achieved

Goals should be broken down into time frames, such as:

- Immediate goals—In the next ninety days, what are the top three, measurable, realistic targets of accomplishment for your ministry?

    Examples:

    - Advertise for a full-time youth pastor, write a job description, collect resumes, conduct interviews and make recommendation to the leadership team.
    - Finalize the new logo; print new stationary and business cards
    - Start five new small groups

- Short Term—In the next zero to two years, what are the top three, measurable, realistic targets of accomplishment?

  Examples:

  - Locate and acquire a ten-acre site where we can build our permanent facility.
  - Average weekly attendance of 500 plus
  - Increase giving
  - Thirty small groups up and running
  - Hire a pastor of assimilation

- Mid-Range Goals—In the next two to five years, what are the most important, realistic, measurable targets of accomplishment?

  Examples:

  - Design, finance, and build our first facility on our new property
  - Hire a teaching pastor and transition to team teaching model
  - Take staff and ministry leaders for supplemental training
  - Increase attendance to 1,000 per weekend

- Long-Range Goals—In the next five to ten years, what are the most important, realistic, measurable targets of accomplishment?

Examples:

- Launch video venues and satellite campus in areas around the county
- Attendance over 1,500 per weekend
- Build phase two—Family Life Center and expand Worship Center

While there is no right or wrong answer as to how many goals you have in each category, keep them manageable and realistic. I worked with a pastor of a small church in central Wyoming who insisted that his first phase building needed to seat 3,000 people. At the time, his church was running 300 per weekend and not filling the building they had. When I questioned the feasibility of a 3,000-seat worship facility in central Wyoming, the pastor chided me for not having enough faith. That was more than ten years ago and, to this day, the church has not grown beyond 300 people. I don't think my level of faith was the issue. Reality was the issue.

Do This: Work with your leadership team to create relevant and simple Purpose, Mission and Vision statements. Then follow them up with core values. Be praying about the vision God has given you for your church!

Don't Do That: Hope that things will just work themselves out naturally. Be wordy and long-winded, and use "Christianese" code. Avoid writing a mission statement and clear plan. Lie about your core values. Set unreachable goals and let them go unnoticed when one is reached.

LIGHTHOUSE COMMUNITY CHURCH

Purpose
To advance the Kingdom of God
by winning people to Christ,
growing people in Christ,
and sending people to serve
Christ- all to the glory of God.

MISSION
WIN! GROW! EQUIP! SEND!

PRIORITIES
1. Worship
2. Scripture
3. Prayer
4. Evangelism
5. Discipleship
6. Fellowship
7. Ministry
8. Stewardship

KEY STRATEGY
- Come to Church
- Acknowledge Jesus
- Attend Worship
- Learn the Fundamentals
- Join a Relational Group
- Become Involved in
  Christian Education
- Participate in Ministry
- Become a leader

MINISTRY PLANS

KINGDOM PERSON PROFILE
- Knows Christ personally
- Is growing spiritually
- Understands their faith
- Is involved in the life of the church
- Uses their gifts in ministry
- Shares their faith effectively
- Gives of their time and resources
  generously

Core Values
Commitment to Jesus
Biblically focused, culturally relevant
Target focused ministry
Atmosphere of acceptance
Agree to disagree
Ministry before programs
The church as a means, not an end
Message vs. method
Focus on ministry, not facilities
Every member a minister
Commitment to a strong home base
Simple structure
Authority and responsibility
Resource bridge
Focus on church health
Preaching and teaching
Champion led vision
Transformational environment
Global Mission
Ministry/Relationship

CHURCH VISION
We want to be a church that:
- Focuses on Bible teaching, Spirit-led worship,
  and Christ centered community
- Extends God's kingdom by bringing people
  into a relationship with Jesus, producing mature
  disciples, and impacting our culture with the love
  and truth of Christ
- Grows to be a regional, multi-congregation church
  that produces ministries and churches that extend
  God's kingdom

TEN YEAR GOALS
- Growing Regional Church
- Leadership Development Center
- Multi-congregational
- Resource Bridging
- Church Multiplication
- Life Long Biblical Learning
- Community Through Relationship Groups

Tactical Planning

About ten years ago, I worked with a church located in Rochester, New York, called First Bible Baptist Church (FBBC). This church had a regular attendance of 700 people per weekend and was looking to remodel and expand their facilities on North Greece Road. One of my recommendations for the church was to conduct a survey within the church to identify common characteristics of church members. Following the survey, I worked with the pastor and staff to compile and analyze the information. Here is what we found after averaging all of the statstics and inventing a fictious couple to represent a member of FBBC:

A profile of Bob and Barbara Bible-Baptist:

Bob and Barbara are a two income family, with both working as middle managers for Kodak or Xerox. They are raising teenage kids, have a combined income of $80,000.00, drive status symbol cars, and owe $30,000 on credit cards. Bob and Barbara are just a few paychecks away from bankruptcy at any given time. Currently, Kodak and Xerox are laying off middle managers. Stress levels are high at the Bible-Baptist home. Bob and Barbara attend church at least three weekends per month and live within five miles of the church's property.

Once we had gathered this information, we then looked at the community demographics within a five-mile radius of the church's site. Our goal was to identify the number of households in that defined area matching the description of Bob and Barbara Bible-Baptist. Our demographics team reported there were more than 5,000 thousand households in our target area just like Bob and Barbara. We knew that if Bob and Barbara had clearly defined needs, then the thousands of other households we identified would have similar needs.

Next, our programs team went to work and identified or developed various programs to help Bob and Barbara in their quest to live a peaceful, productive life. Here are a few of those programs:

- Crown Ministries for financial management. (Today we would use Dave Ramsey's Financial Peace University.) If Bob and Barbara could get out of debt, their life would be more peaceful.
- Classes were developed to help Bob and Barbara deal with raising teenage children.
- Marriage counseling options were highlighted and provided.
- Job training and career classes were developed and brought in.
- Sports activities were formed around softball, soccer, and other activities for kids and adults.
- To relieve stress, a paintball program was formed, utilizing the church's many acres of forest!

These represent just a few of the programs and ministries formed to meet the real life needs of Bob and Barbara. FBBC was able to offer these programs not only to Bob and Barbara, but also to the several thousand households within the church's target area. The communications team was then tasked with advertising the various programs and ministries to those in the target area.

The response from the community was overwhelming! So overwhelming in fact, the church quickly outgrew their facilities. In November of 2004, FBBC purchased ninety acres on Manitou Road and began planning for the construction of a new and larger ministry center. The new facility was completed in September of 2007. Today, FBBC continues to be a strong, growing, and healthy church, training Christ-like disciples for ministry in Rochester and around the world.

As you look to take your ministry to the next level, take a good look at the people your ministry is attracting. Who visits your church and what are they like? Of the weekly visitors, who comes back and who gets involved? If your church attracts the young Mosaics (what Barna calls the eighteen- to twenty-seven-year-olds), then you should focus on the needs of that group and put a lot (but not all) of your effort into reaching them. I have found churches trying to be everything to everyone rarely succeed. Once you have a clear picture of who you are as a church congregation, and you have identified your target demographically, culturally, geographically, and spiritually, then develop the ministries and programs needed to best serve your church and the community God has entrusted to you.

Following my work with First Bible Baptist Church, I went on to work with hundreds of other churches using the same steps. Warning, wimps need not apply for the task of creating a Strategic Ministry Plan. There is a lot of work involved in developing a Strategic Ministry Plan. If you are one of those pastors who operate his ministry out of some denominational handbook, or off the pages of some air-tight job description, you are not going to like this and will probably never do it anyway. However, if you are committed to giving God your best, to developing the best plan and to building the best ministry that God desires for you, then you will most likely enjoy this process.

In 2008, I had the privilege of working with Pastor John Snyder at Crossroads Community Church in Parker, Colorado.

Crossroads was running about 400 to 500 people on a weekend. John, along with staff and volunteers, did an outstanding job in the development of their Strategic Ministry Plan. John did not do all this work alone. We recruited, trained, and helped various teams who gathered and assimilated the needed information. We will get into the details of teams and tasks later on. I have included the findings from the various teams we established, along with a link to the twenty-six, ministry-specific MAPS.

The Ministry Action Plans (Maps)

Taking a large cross section of Crossroads Community Church members, we administered a very extensive survey, from which we discovered a lot about the people of the church. We also purchased a demographic study of people living within a ten-mile radius of the church. From this information, we learned a lot about who had already been reached through various programs and ministries, and we learned how to pray for those in our community we still want to reach. The attributes we've learned about our target demographic have been summed up in the characters of Carl and Carol. The following demonstrates what we know about these people:

Taken from Crossroads Community Church Strategic Ministry Plan. To see the complete plan go to www. bradoaster.com

- Carl and Carol have attended Crossroads for about two years.
- Carl and Carol are probably forty years old.
- Carl and Carol have been Christians for about nine years.
- Carl and Carol felt attracted to Crossroads because of the strong biblical teaching and feel they are growing spiritually right now.

- Carl and Carol likely both have a college degree.
- As a couple, they are making a decent living, somewhere between $50,000 and $100,000 a year, and one of them is self-employed.
- Carl and Carol give 3 to 6 percent of their income to charitable causes, including the church and other organizations. One of them at least volunteers in a shelter or other non-profit organization from time to time.
- Carl and Carol live within five miles of Crossroads.
- Carl and Carol have two to three children who range in age from nursery to high school. Their children attend public school and enjoy our Children's and Youth Ministry programs at Crossroads.
- Carl and Carol understand and agree with the purpose of the church and are involved in some aspect of ministry, like a small group or volunteer service.
- There are many at Crossroads who are older or younger than Carl and Carol, who are brand new Christians or have known Christ even longer than they have.
- Part of the *crowd, congregation,* and *committed.*

Our People—
Who We Hope to Reach

Taking the same cross section, we combined the attributes of the demographics we hope to reach in the characters of Douglas and Elberta County.

- Doug and Elberta earn about the same amount of annual income as Carl and Carol.

- Doug and Elberta believe in God, but may be part of 50 percent of people in our community who say they don't believe God is actively involved in our world.
- Doug and Elberta may be part of the 50 percent who also say they have dropped out of church and have no desire for God, but may be part of the 50 percent who are still open to God and His work in their lives.
- Doug and Elberta desire to preserve the traditional family structure and, in spite of their possible skepticism about God, still see the role of the church in forming and supporting the development of moral values.
- Doug and Elberta live within a ten-mile radius of the church, along with more than 109,000 other people. There are tens of thousands of Doug's and Alberta's within our reach who need Christ.
- Doug and Elberta are part of the *community* and *crowd*.

Our Potential—What We Believe God Will Do

The extent of our reach is based on the following underlying facts:

- In 2004, the average attendance at Crossroads was 230.
- In 2005, the average attendance was 347. In 2006, the average attendance was 491. In 2007, 604. In the first few months of 2008, attendance reached 727. Growth rate = 23-51 percent/yr.
- Over 100 people have come to Christ as Lord and Savior in the past four years.
- In the first two months of 2008, at least fourteen people received Christ.

- God is calling us to shepherd and care for more and more people within our community and we need to do all we can to be prepared to care for them.
- If God continues to grow Crossroads by just 20 percent each year for the next five years, our average attendance in 2012 will be 1,504.

Our Predicament— Obstacles to Overcome

There are at least three major obstacles in the way of us keeping up with all that God is doing at Crossroads. As you know, there are good problems (like not enough room for everyone who is coming) and bad problems (like not having enough people or money to take care of the building and property we do have). The problems listed below are good problems to have, but still they are problems we need to overcome. In the section entitled "Our Plans," we share how we hope to overcome these obstacles.

Obstacle #1: Our Facility

As God sends more and more people, we have maxed out our facility. We don't have enough seats in the auditorium for all who are going to come in the near future. We have neither enough room in our nursery for all the babies, or enough classroom space for all the toddlers through fifth graders. Our facility is also very old and in many ways does not meet the present building codes of the town of Parker. We have not had to meet codes because our facility was here before the town of Parker was incorporated, so we are protected by a "grandfather" policy, but our present and projected growth mandates that we take these things into account as we plan for the future. For instance, at this time, our facility makes use of a well and septic system. We will need to tap into the town of Parker water and sewer system as we plan to grow.

Obstacle #2: Our Property

We presently own a little less than two and a quarter acres of land. That is almost twice as much as we owned in May of 2006, but in June of that year we did choose to purchase the 1.08 acres north of us. We cannot significantly increase the size of our building because if we do, we will not have enough parking to meet code. If we are to stay at our present location, we need to be able to come up with a way to acquire more land here, add more weekend services, or find some other creative way to include people at offsite locations. No matter how we look at it, the amount of land we own is an obstacle to us keeping up with what God is doing.

Obstacle #3: Our Staff

Church experts agree that the best functioning churches have one full-time ministry staff member for every 120 to 150 people in attendance on any given Sunday. And again, most church experts say it is best to hire staff to grow to the next level instead of waiting to get to the next level and then hiring staff. (For example, if you have 450, you should start looking for a fourth staff member; don't wait until you are at 600 to hire a fourth.).

Right now, we have four full-time ministry staff, with an attendance of almost 700 on Sundays. If we put one full-time ministry staff member for every 120 attendees then we should have six full-time ministry staff members. If we go with one ministry staff member for every 150 then we should have five on staff right now and in the process of hiring a sixth staff member soon.

Our Plans

Our Ministry Action Plans (MAPs) for 2008 are outlined below:

(To see the detailed reports of the MAPs, please go to www.bradoaster.com)

- Senior Pastor
- Sunday Growth MAP
- Future Staff Hiring MAP
- Future Facility and Land Expansion
- Adult Ministry Pastor
- Small Group Ministry MAP
- First Impressions Team MAP
- Community Outreach/Missions MAP
- Youth Ministry Pastor
- FUSION (Middle School Ministry) MAP
- ELEVATION (High School Ministry) MAP
- Children's Ministry Director
- Toddler Ministry Hiring MAP
- Elementary Ministry MAP
- Vacation Bible School MAP
- Women's Ministry Director
- Women's Leadership Team MAP
- Men's Ministry Director

- Men's Leadership Team MAP
- Office Manager
- Volunteer Office Workers MAP
- Visitor Follow Up MAP
- Crossroads Café/Events
- Crossroads Café/Events Team MAP

2008 MAP for Sunday Morning Growth

Senior Pastor

Our projected Sunday morning average attendance for 2008 is 725. We already averaged 727 in the first six weeks of the year. We could very possibly be averaging over 800 in late spring and in late fall of 2008. Our parking lot is often already full at the 9:30 a.m. and 11:00 a.m. services. Statistics show that when a church auditorium is 80 percent full, the attendance plateaus or declines. The auditorium "feels" full once 80 percent of the seats are full. Our auditorium presently seats 325. Eighty percent of 325 is 260. If we fill our auditorium during both the 9:30 and 11:00 services, we would have 520 in the auditorium for those two services, with possibly another 100 in our 8:00 service, for a total adult attendance of 620.

If the attendance in the auditorium typically makes up 70 percent of our Sunday attendance, then, realistically, once we get to a total attendance of 875, we will max out both the 9:30 and 11:00 service and get 100 in the auditorium at 8:00 a.m. At our current growth trend, we will average

870 by the end of 2009. Parking may keep us from reaching this attendance. Room for Children's Ministry Classes may limit this growth. We need to come up with some options to spread out our parking and our attendance.

Seats in auditorium	80% of seats – when church "feels" full	Both 9:30 and 11:00 at 80%	8:00 at 100 in attendance in auditorium	Children at 30% of total attendance	Realistic max attendance in 3 services
325	260	520	100	265	885

Goals

- Come up with a plan for more parking on Sunday mornings.
- Come up with a way to make room for the additional people who want to come for worship, and for their children.

Plan for Goal #1—plan for more parking on Sunday mornings

- Put a Parking Task Force together by April 1. Their job will be to come up with at least three plans for either expanding our parking or setting up alternative parking arrangements (such as off-site parking with shuttle service).Come up with a way to make room for the additional people who want to come for worship, and for their children.

- Ask the Task Force to present at least three alternative plans to the CLC by June 9 with the goal of implementing the approved plan by August 17, 2008.

Plan for Goal #2—making room for additional people

- Our Land Investigation Team has been working on recommendations for this.

(To read the full SMP with all MAPS included go to: www.bradoaster.com)

In 2009, John and the staff developed and rolled out their "Declaration of Dependence" to the congregation. This is a great way to share your church's core beliefs with your congregation and bring a higher sense of unity. I would encourage your church to consider adding some statement of core beliefs to your Strategic Ministry Plan.

Crossroads Community Church

Declaration of Dependence
Under our God, we seek to fulfill this sense of purpose.
Crossroads is an embracing community of believers, committed to encouraging people to experience a life-changing, love relationship with God.
Under our God, we seek to live out these core values:
God
We seek to honor God through worship and prayer
You
We believe everyone matters to God

Relationships

We believe relationships allow extraordinary things to happen!

Encouragement

We know an encouraging community is essential in helping people live for God.

Authenticity

We promote authenticity by being open and honest with God, each other, and ourselves.

Leadership

We honor those in leadership because they are accountable to God.

Excellence

We offer God the best in all we do.

Relevance

We commit to being relevant by using ever-changing methods to communicate the never changing message.

Under Our God, We Seek to Accomplish This Task

We believe our God-given mission for the next four to six years is to develop a larger campus with larger facilities to better minister to those God has sent us while developing ministries to touch, with the love of Jesus, the hearts of those who would not typically come into a church building.

Under God We Make These Wholehearted Commitments

As we attempt to fulfill our God-given purpose, we make these three wholehearted commitments to God, to His people, and to those who do not yet know Jesus:

We will never compromise our sense of purpose in our attempt to fulfill our sense of mission.

We will never compromise our heartfelt values in our attempt to fulfill our mission.

We will never compromise our biblical beliefs and convictions in our attempt to fulfill our sense of mission.

Above all else, we will always honor our God and His ways and will always seek to be like our Savior, Jesus Christ, in how we treat, live with, pray for, and interact with others.

———◆◆◆———

John Snyder, his staff, and the ministry teams at Crossroads Community Church did an outstanding job in developing their Strategic Ministry Plan. That being said, no SMP is worth the paper it is written on, if it is not implemented, monitored, improved upon, and updated on a regular basis. Developing a

SMP only to put it up on the shelf is like wetting your pants in a dark suit. It gives you a warm feeling, but nobody notices!

A Strategic Ministry Plan is a living, breathing document that needs to be reviewed for progress, used as an evaluation tool, referred to at staff and board meetings and updated regularly with new strategies, goals, and objectives. By the way, there is nothing more demoralizing for you, your staff, and volunteers than to accomplish a major goal and feel like no one even noticed. I encourage you to go to the extreme, looking for reasons to celebrate even the smallest of victories. Do the unexpected when someone overcomes a challenge or completes a task. I made the mistake, early in my career, of thinking that I had to do something big for someone in order to make a reward worthwhile. As a result, I rarely did anything. Big mistake. Simple recognition of a job well done is often enough to encourage someone and let them know that their effort is appreciated. Lunch with a pastor or some other one-on-one activity would be great.

Do This: Know your congregation. Do in-depth research to see who is there, who might come if invited, and who you'd like to have in your congregation. Work hard and operate at the highest level possible. Look for the people you want to reach, the potential you have, and acknowledging problems as well as solutions. Create Ministry Action Plans (MAPS) for each goal and each specific ministry within your church. Keep the plan simple. Envision your future and be determined to get there. Write down your church's core values. Keep your goals measurable, realistic, and reward yourself when you achieve them.

Don't Do That: Pay no mind to the congregation and their specific needs or desires. Strictly follow a job description and do not deviate from it. Grumble about the need for change but stay idle.

Developing Your Facility Development Plan

Have you ever heard the statement, "If you are a hammer, everything you see looks like a nail"? That phrase accurately described me for many years. Every church I met, in my opinion, needed a new facility. They should either be looking at a major remodel, an addition to the existing building, another building on their campus, or they should be acquiring land and expanding elsewhere. For many years, I was a hammer, in search of something to nail!

Every time I get to the point where I honestly believe I can say I have seen it all, God surprises me by exposing me to yet another way in which He can grow His church. The secret to successfully growing your church is acknowledging it's God's church. Look to God for His plan and then follow it! Not really rocket science, is it?

The reasons why so many churches fail in their attempts at facility planning are plentiful. Have you ever watched David Letterman? I usually get a kick out of his Top Ten list. Here are my top ten reasons why churches fail when facility planning:

- The first thing the church leadership does is contact an architect.
- They have no strategic plan, purpose, sense of direction or goal.

- Someone with an office and overhead leads the church in the wrong direction. (This could be a realtor, architect, builder, design/build firm, consultant, or anyone else who stands to gain financially from building a new facility.)
- The pastor has an ego that will only fit in a very large facility with a certain number of seats.
- Church leadership is guided by an elder or building committee member who has no idea what he or she is talking about, but says things to impress others.
- The church must keep up with the church down the street so no members are lost to that church.
- The church depends on a new facility to attract new people, rather than focus on quality programs and ministries.
- Church leaders think building programs will unify an otherwise dysfunctional congregation.
- A really nice facility will help the church attract and keep quality staff.
- Church leadership believes the entire church should be able to meet all together in one service.

Churches from all over the country have called on a regular basis and explained to me why they need to expand their facilities. Most of those churches are correct, but do not know the best way to go about expanding their facilities. Before we get into the details of acquiring raw land, working with architects, city or county agencies, hiring a builder, and everything else you will need to know when building from scratch, let's explore other options that might work for your church. We'll give you actual examples of what different churches have done, for better or worse, so that you can learn from their experience and build upon it.

To Build or Not to Build?

I believe that whenever you are given various options that lead to the fulfillment of an objective, it is best to go with the safest option if at all possible. An option that presents an opportunity for lower cost and lower risk is always worth exploring. Here is a list of options that you should consider when looking to expand your facilities.

Let's look at a start-up church meeting in a temporary location such as a school:

- Can you continue to grow by relocating within the temporary space? If meeting at a school, can you move from the cafeteria to the gym? Can you utilize more classrooms?
- Can you relocate to a better, temporary space like the YMCA or a community center within your target area? Maybe another school would cut you a better deal or provide you with better space?
- Can you lease space in an office park, shopping center, or other space that is friendly to Christian ministries?
- Have you checked out empty warehouse space? You may be able to occupy part and use part for storage sites.

The goal here is to stay focused on your ministry and not get distracted with a building program until absolutely necessary.

Now let's look at churches that own their facilities but are running tight on space.

- Can you remodel your existing facility in order to better utilize the space you already have?
- Can you upgrade your existing facility and add new space by adding on to your existing facility?

- Can you tear down an older, single story part of your facility and replace it with a multi-level facility? Multi-level buildings provide more space and do not take up anymore land than single story buildings.
- Can you bring in temporary space like modular buildings? Move your staff offices and other uses that are non-essential to Sunday morning activities into the modular's and expand your ministries into the vacated office space.
- Can you move your staff offices off-site and use the vacated space for expansion?
- Using a phased development approach, can you systematically tear down your entire facility and rebuild new on your current site?
- Can you buy up properties that border your site, homes, raw land, etc., and use those properties for ministry expansion?

Let's say that you have exhausted all possible expansion ideas and are forced to move to a new location. Before you buy land and commit to building from scratch, consider this:

- Can you purchase an existing structure such as an old Wal-Mart, Home Depot, Shopping Center, or other Big Box building? According to Colliers International, there is currently 300 million square feet or 34 percent of large format retail space now sitting empty!
- With 3,000 churches closing every year, can you acquire an existing church facility and update it?
- Can you take over an existing "large church" facility from a failing ministry?
- Can you acquire a large sports facility, community center, or other existing facility for your ministry expansion?
- Can you partner with an existing "Christian school" and build a multipurpose facility on their property?

- Can you lease land from a public school and build a multipurpose facility on the leased land?

Here are a few examples of creative facility solutions that give much needed space while minimizing cost and risk.

Mountain Vista Church, Mesa, Arizona: Pastor Rich Wisley, after meeting at a school for years, leased 10,000 square feet in an industrial park. The space was a large, unfinished shell and required $400,000 worth of improvements before the church could use it. The owner of the building put up half the money and the church paid for the rest. Rich also has an option to acquire additional space in the building as needed.

First Southern Baptist Church of Fountain Valley, California, added an entire second floor to their existing school. This was accomplished during a three-month window in the summer when school was not in session. As the first floor was never designed to carry the load of a second floor, the addition was built upon a structure that completely spanned the existing building.

Bethany Assembly, Everett, Washington, developed a multi-phased approach, including a major remodel and reallocation of space, along with several future additions to the existing facility. Today, what once was an outdated and tired looking facility has a modern, state of the art look, and it facilitates a growing and contemporary ministry.

Each of these churches started out wanting me to help them build new facilities, some at their current location and some on new sites. Through the process of developing their Strategic Ministry Plans, God opened their eyes to new ideas and, in some cases, a new way of thinking. Each ministry accomplished their goal of providing additional space for their expanding ministries without building new facilities on undeveloped property. While most architects and builders will want you to build new facilities on raw land, that is not always the best option for your ministry. By the way, every church I listed above is running over one thousand people per weekend, some over ten thousand!

Born-Again Facilities

As churches across the country look to expand their ministries through video venues and off-site locations, many are caught in the never-ending problem of entitlement issues, use permits, and the neighbors. To side-step these challenges, we suggest you consider a new process called "Facility Evangelism."

Back when I was growing up in the San Francisco Bay Area, land prices were just beginning to soar. In addition, the local and state governments were making new construction more and more difficult by ramping up regulations. Agencies like the Coastal Commission, Sierra Club, and others were joining with local city and county agencies, intentionally making new development unlikely and very expensive. I recall back in the late seventies a restaurant was attempting to build a new location on the beach in Pacifica, California. Putting a new building structure close to the beach would set off years of entitlement issues, environmental impact reports, neighborhood meetings, and more. After years of battling city hall for a new permit, they eventually tried a new approach. The company bought an old restaurant in a good location just down the beach. This restaurant had been in existence for a long time. The existing building was dilapidated and of little or no value. That is unless you consider what it had other than physical form: a use permit, a great location on the beach, an established use, existing utility hook ups, and no environmental issues. Other than being a D8 building (get a D8 Caterpillar tractor and knock it over), it was a great find and solved many of the new restaurants problems!

Now, if you were to buy the existing property, you could tear down the old building and build a new one on the same site, but you would have to comply with all the same regulations necessary for new construction. Why bother with all that fuss? Rather than tearing it down, if you apply for an "addition/remodel" permit, you can side-step all the "new construction" issues. That is exactly what the restaurant did in Pacifica. It was the most impressive "addition/remodel" project that I had ever seen. The new owner of the old restaurant simply built a brand new restaurant right over the top of the old one and then proceeded to gut the old one from the inside of the new one! Legally, all they had to do was keep one section of one wall from the old building and the project was considered an addition/remodel!

This type of development became very popular in the 80s and 90s as more and more regulations were put into place to control new construction. It was very common to see a real estate developer side-step difficult and costly regulations by purchasing an old home, tearing down all but one section of one wall and then building a huge mansion on the same site. As church development becomes more difficult (and even more expensive), churches who are expanding through off-site video venues are looking to redevelop old churches in the same manner. Old, tired church buildings often sit on great locations. With the average size of an off-site venue being around 500 seats, many of these old facilities can be bought cheap and redeveloped into "born again" ministry centers without all the fuss and hassle normally associated with new construction.

The BIG BOX Option

Let's take a quick look at the benefits of buying a "big box" building like my friend, Greg Rollinger, at Palm Valley Community Church purchased in Goodyear, Arizona. At the time, I had helped Greg with his long-range Strategic Ministry Plan. The church had purchased forty acres west of Phoenix and things were on track toward development of the first phase. When an empty furniture store (an existing big box building) became available, it offered huge advantages over the custom designed, build from scratch option.

The build from scratch, custom design for Palm Valley required:

- Land to be purchased
- The land needed rezoning for church use
- Utilities had to be brought to the property
- The site had to be engineered by a civil engineer
- Off-site work was needed, including streets, curbs, gutters, sidewalks, traffic lights, etc.
- Storm Water Management Plan had to be developed
- Soils reports were needed
- Environmental Impact Reports were called for
- Traffic studies were needed
- Architects were necessary for building designs
- Planning Department approval of designs
- Neighborhood meetings need to take place
- Structural engineers were needed to design structural systems for the building
- Mechanical, electrical, and plumbing designs were mandated
- Landscaping had to be designed and installed
- Signage permits and signs were needed.
- A general contractor was needed to build the facility and do the site work

There is more, but I think you get the point!

Now, let's look at common risks involved in custom design/build from scratch:

- The site work and land development costs are often unaffordable

- Cities can be uncooperative in issuing permits
- Unexpected environmental issues can come up, increasing the development costs
- The architect designs what you cannot afford to build
- The city traffic engineer requires expensive, off-site improvements
- The builder clobbers you with never-ending change orders
- The construction process takes much longer than you expect
- The landscape architect designs a "Garden of Eden," costing a fortune to install and maintain

And yes, there are more risks involved, but again, I am sure you get my point!

Then, of course, there is the cost to consider. A new church facility in the greater Phoenix area would cost around 130 dollars per square foot. Looking at a 1,000-seat, sixty thousand square foot facility, the cost would amount to 7.8 million dollars. Site work to accommodate parking, landscaping, storm water, underground utilities, and off-site work, pedestrian and traffic circulation will likely add another three million dollars. Soft costs such as design fees, building permits, interest on the construction loan, utility hook up fees, contingencies, and other miscellaneous expenses can add another two million dollars. With the tax and tip included, we are now in the range of 12,800,000 dollars for the custom designed building.

Now, let's look at what is already done for you when you buy an existing "big box."

- Because you are buying it and not building it, you know the price up front.
- The building comes with the land! (And usually a better location than raw land.)
- No need for civil engineer or landscape designer! The property already has all site improvements completed,

landscaping, parking lot, utilities, storm water, street improvements, sidewalks, etc.

- No soils report or EIR are needed.
- Generally, a sign comes with the building.
- An empty box is costing someone a lot of money and they will usually sell it for less than it cost to build.
- Most, but not all, of your risk has already been mitigated by the original developer.
- You can be in this building much faster than if you built a custom facility. Not weeks faster, but years faster.

Many of these empty "big boxes" can be bought for around $75 per square foot. While that price includes land, site work, and building, typically the building is a wide-open shell. To build out a church facility within the completed shell, you will likely spend another $45 per square foot before you can move in. (That amount usually covers the design fees and permits.) Using the numbers from above, a 60,000 square foot building would cost 4.5 million dollars to buy (at $75 per square foot). The interior build out cost another $2.7 million (60,000 sq/ft x $45) for a total of $7.2 million. Now you might be tempted to compare that number to the $12.8 million above, but the $12.8 million does not include the cost of the land whereas the $7.2 million does! And don't forget the risk you have also avoided.

Let me say this loud and clear: do not build a new church facility on raw land if you do not need to! You will lower your risk, save time and money, and most often end up in a better location by buying an existing, empty, "big box" building. In addition, you can almost always add onto the big box should you outgrow it! Your congregation will applaud your economical approach to ministry expansion and the value you put on the funds they donate! You will be able to spend a lot more time focusing on the needs of people, expanding the ministry, and having fun with your family.

Beware of the "Good Deal"

A pastor of Calvary Assembly in Milpitas, California, called one day and his voice was filled with excitement. His church had sold their existing property that fronted Highway 680 to a real estate developer, taken the cash from the sale and bought a beautiful new site on the corner of Calaveras Blvd. and Piedmont Road. I met with the pastor later that day at the new property and it was indeed beautiful. When the pastor told me what the church had paid for the land, it sounded too good to be true. Obviously I believed the pastor, but why would land this nice sell for that low of a price?

Turns out, the man who sold them the land was an old, Indian fellow who had lived on the property. As I investigated the site for the proposed church development, here is what I discovered:

> The city of Milpitas would require Calvary to realign the intersection in front of the church to form a four-way intersection.
>
> Realigning one of the roads meant the church was building a new road along the western border of their new property.
>
> At the new intersection, Calvary would need to install a "four-way" controlled intersection including all traffic lights.

One of the roads would cross a drainage area that controlled water runoff for the 100-year floor plan. Calvary would have to build a bridge over that runoff canal.

In addition to the bridge, Calvary would have to line the canal with riprap for erosion control. The erosion control would need to extend to the East side of the new bridge for about half a mile.

On the property was an old "Spanish Adobe." It was historical, so Calvary could not tear it down. The Spanish Adobe had to be brought up to current codes and made handicap accessible!

There was no sewer line.

A sound wall had to be constructed as the church was up against a neighborhood.

The new sound wall caused heat to be trapped in twelve of the neighboring homes, and the residents demanded the city have Calvary put air conditioning in those homes.

The parking lot would be sitting directly on an a major earthquake fault line!

And lastly, as part of the design preparation, I needed to do a soils report to see what kind of dirt we would be building on top of. To conduct a soils report, you drill down to the bedrock and analyze the different types and compaction of soils at different levels. The drill went down about five feet and started spitting up bones, lots and lots of bones! Calvary had literally bought an Indian burial ground! The experts that were brought in estimated that there were 2,000 dead Indians buried on the property dating back in time to the crusades! In the end, soil had to be moved to cover the burial ground so that the shallowest grave was two feet deeper than the deepest footing.

Calvary had already sold their former facility and spent the money they received on the new property. The seller of the property knew it was an Indian burial ground and disclosed it to the pastor in a document buried in boxes and boxes of stuff he had turned over to the church during the escrow period. No one from the church ever read all of the documents until it was too late, and escrow had closed.

Had I been the pastor, I would have sold the new property to the city of Milpitas for a regional park. If they would not buy the property from me, I would have donated it to them.

Next, I would have asked the developer to sell me back the old church site. In the long run, it would have been cheaper and faster to give the land to the city, buy the old property back for twice what the developer paid for it and eventually build new facilities on the property fronting the freeway. The church did not do that. Rather, they moved back to a school and spent ten years and millions of dollars mitigating one issue after another until eventually they were able to build a small facility, which, in my opinion, is no better than the one they sold.

Do This: Check all options and opportunities. List all requirements for facility planning as well as the risks. Choose the option that best fits your church and MAP. Carefully look into every "good deal," assessing all of the risks involved.

Don't Do That: Go with the first plan you think of and run with it. Go with the lowest-cost option, not paying attention to the risk. Build a new church facility without considering renovation first. Take the good deals that cross your path.

Creative Land Acquisition

How do churches go about acquiring land today? How do they compete for property when land prices are continuing to climb? Competition for good sites is putting property out of financial reach at a time when more and more ministries need to expand their facilities. I have found that if you can't win at a particular game, the best strategy is to change the rules or reinvent the game so that you *can* win. And not only win at the game, but also give yourself an advantage over all the other players!

The typical approach to land acquisition usually goes something like this:

> Community Christian Church (CCC) has outgrown its existing site. They meet at a local high school and are really, really tired of the set-up, takedown, and hassle of dealing with a temporary facility. The church is running an average attendance of 450 and has a general operating budget of $500,000. Following the summer slump, they are currently $21,000 behind in their budget. The decision to buy land and build a permanent facility is made, and a task force is established to acquire twenty acres suitable for the development. A land broker is contacted, interviewed, and hired to find a site for the church. After a short time, three sites have been located and are presented to the church.
>
> Site #1—A twenty-acre site is located just ten minutes from where the church currently meets. Zoning is

agricultural, and the owner has it listed for $40,000 per acre. There is no city water or sewer to the site, and the street will need to be improved. The county will allow church use in an agricultural zone. With the land cost of $800,000 and site improvement costs (utilities, street improvements, and grading) of $500,000, the twenty-acre site will cost $1,300,000.

Challenge—At a cost of $1,300,000, CCC would need to use the entire proceeds from a three-year capital stewardship fund drive just to acquire the land and provide the site improvements. This is assuming that CCC could raise three times its annual budget over three years! The church could borrow the money either from a bank or through a bond program, but could not afford the payments, which would equal one-third of their operating budget.

Site #2—A twenty-three-acre site within the city limits is located. This site has water, power, and sewer to the property and is located at a prime intersection near the regional mall. Zoning is commercial and all street improvements are in. Cost: $75,000 per acre, for a total of $1,725,000.

Challenge—Great site, but Bill Gates doesn't attend CCC!

Site #3—Eighteen acres of land are located in a light-industrial part of town. Utilities and street improvements are in and the land is cheap, at $32,000 per acre. Total cost: $576,000.

Challenge—Getting the city to allow a church in a light industrial area will require a variance from the city council, and the future development of daycare or school facilities would not be allowed. Although the price is reasonable, do members of CCC or potential visitors want to drive through an industrial area on Sunday morning to go to church? This part of town is not in the path of future development and would continue to decline.

This scenario is typical of what most churches end up looking at when they rely on a real estate broker to go out and find property for them. Most brokers simply look at the MLS (multiple listing service) to see what is available and then bring those listings to the church. The problem is, all the good deals never make it to the MLS. Real estate developers buy them up long before the brokers are ever aware the property is for sale. What is left are sites like the three above—land that is unaffordable, undevelopable, and undesirable.

So how do you find land for your church? To start out, we have to agree on some simple facts:

- The owner of all land is God
- Lost people matter to God
- The church exists to reach lost people
- Churches need land
- God has land for churches

These facts being true, then whether or not the land is currently for sale does not need to be an obstacle!

What land is suitable for the work of a church? Only the best. After all, God owns all the land, and the bride of Christ is the church, so why would God want His bride to settle for anything less than the best?

So Where Is the Best Land?

To determine the best land for a church, we have to look at property, not at what it is today, but at what it will become tomorrow. God knows what will happen in the future. He can foresee the development of your community and knows where to best locate your church, based on future development and future ministry opportunities. So, to understand where God wants your church to be, you have to understand the future development of your community.

Here are several examples of how I have been able to help churches acquire property in a way that can only be described as "a God thing!"

A young start-up church in Gilbert, Arizona, had been meeting in a high school. After the church completed its Strategic Ministry Plan, they determined a permanent site of fifteen acres was needed for the long-term goals of their ministry. The church had 300 members, a $250,000 general budget, was slightly behind on giving, with no cash on hand for land acquisition.

The land acquisition team located an eighty-acre parcel just inside the city limits. The property cost about $800,000 and was in the direct path of development as the city continued to grow. The church drafted an offer to buy the eighty acres and submited the offer to the owner, along with an earnest money check in the amount of $10,000. (The land acquisition team and church leadership raised the money.) The offer was accepted, and a ninety-day escrow account was opened. Upon closing, the church would need to pay for the property in full. Did I mention that the church had no money? Raising the earnest money was a challenge!

Prior to the church presenting the purchase offer, the land acquisition team identified a potential buyer for sixty-five of the eighty acres. It turned out the city of Gilbert's Department of Parks and Recreation was looking for a regional park in the same area but wanted sixty-five acres, not eighty. A deal was made, including having the Department of Parks and Recreation bring the utilities to the site. Upon acceptance of the offer, the church sold sixty-five acres to the city at a higher per acre cost than they had been offered for the entire eighty acres. The result: the church had fifteen acres, paid for, with utilities to the site, and a development agreement allowing the church to use the new park's parking for overflow and had joint use of all park fields. How would you like a church site surrounded on two sides by a brand new regional park?

Superstition Springs Community Church eventually took my advice and changed their name. The church is now known as Mission Community Church. To see the completed site, log onto Google Earth and type in the church address: 4450 E. Elliot Road, Gilbert, Arizona.

Crossroads Bible Church

A thriving Bible Church in Lewisville, Texas, outgrew its existing site and was looking to relocate to fifty acres. The Land Acquisition Team located a sixty-five-acre parcel of land. The land was in a prime location for a regional church looking to serve the fast-growing communities north of the Dallas/Fort Worth area. This time, the property owner was set on a sale price of $1,500,000. The two problems with the site were that the city utilities were a mile away, and the church had no money. So what do you do when the owner won't budge on the $1.5 million price tag and you know it will cost an additional $300,000 to $400,000 to get the utilities to the site? Do you look at other sites? Not if you have prayed about this one and you are convinced that the Owner of all the land wants the church on this site! Here is how the Lord provided the property for this church.

The church secured an option to purchase the land for $1,500,000. Then, fifteen acres on the corner of a future intersection was subdivided and rezoned for a commercial development of mini storage. The church marketed the fifteen-acre site to a Dallas developer who agreed to purchase it for $1,200,000. The developer also agreed to bring all utilities to the site for his development and stub them into the remaining fifty acres for the church! Now there still remained $300,000 on the initial purchase price of the land, but because it was valued at over one million dollars, bank financing was not a problem. The church then initiated a twelve-month capital fund raising program to pay off the land. One year later, the church owned, free and clear, fifty beautiful acres in a prime location.

Looking for land? All you need is an experienced guide and a healthy disregard for conventional thinking! Check out the campus at Crossroads by logging on to Google Earth and typing in this address: 8301 Justin Road, Lewisville, Texas.

Crossroads Grace Community Church

Manteca, California – Pastor Mike Moore and I had worked together for several years developing a strategic ministry plan and looking for a site where the church could relocate and expand their ministry. I told Mike about the incredible things I had seen God do when providing land for His church, and Mike told me God seemed to do those things for others, but he didn't think God would do it for him.

Working with the land acquisition team, I identified a dozen suitable pieces of property for Crossroads. At one meeting, Mike told me that one of the properties we were considering was his favorite. He had walked on the property, praying God would provide it for the church. (What Mike called a prayer walk, others might call trespassing. And when your heavenly Father owns the planet, how much trouble can a pastor get into anyway?)

After hearing about how Mike felt that God had led him to the site, I put it at the top of the list and went after it. If you pull up the site on Google Earth (1505 Moffat Boulevard, Manteca, California), you will see the completed multipurpose center with the red roof. To the north of the church property is a business park.

When the church bought the property, it included all the land north of Moffat and south of the freeway interchange. Crossroads was able to sell off part of the land to the business park developer for more money than it cost to buy all the land! This is just another example of how God goes about providing land for His church in locations He desires.

The secret to creative land acquisition is working directly with landowners, helping them to achieve their goals, and doing it so everyone wins. Years ago I worked with a church in Holland, Michigan. We located a nice piece of property owned by an elderly fellow named Dale. Having lived and farmed the same area all his life, he had acquired a lot of land that was now worth millions of dollars. Dale told me about a deal he had put together for another church that wanted to buy some of his land. Although Dale certainly did not need the money, the property value represented his children's inheritance, and Dale was very protective of it. Dale described the arrangements he had made with the church as follows:

- The twenty-acre site was valued at $1.5 million.
- Dale purchased a life insurance policy on himself, made payable to his children for $1.5 million.
- The church would pay the premium to Dale, who in turn paid the life insurance company.
- The land was gifted to the church so development could start right away.
- When Dale dies, the insurance company pays his children $1.5 million, tax free!

Now Dale was giving the land to the church and the church was building a new facility on it, what if the church failed to make the payments to Dale for the life insurance policy? To protect Dale and to cover all scenarios, the church established an escrow account and deposited the payments into it. The church agreed to always have enough money in the account to cover five years' worth of payments.

The tax free benefits from the life insurance policy offset the appreciation the land would have gained under Dale's ownership, so everyone won! When I told Dale this was exactly the "out of the box" thinking that helps churches acquire land, he replied that his having to die to make this all work sounded more like "in the box" thinking to him!

Remember, look to God to provide the property or facility your ministry needs. If you are looking for land, get an experienced guide and a healthy disregard for conventional thinking. Don't rely on a real estate broker to find land God has reserved for your ministry; realtors just get in the way. All land is for sale, and you will never get what you don't ask for. The best deals always happen when God matches the heart of a pastor with the heart of a landowner. Never settle for less than the best.

Do This: Do in-depth research into the land you want to purchase. Look at it with your church's future plans in mind. Trust God to provide the property or facility you need for your ministry.

Don't Do That: Think "in the box," keeping your eyes focused on the right now. Take everything into your own hands or put it into a realtor's hands. Give the realtor all control when it comes to finding land for your church.

The Transitional Phase of Church Development

Sometimes, in order to get from where you currently are to where you eventually want to be, you need to take more than one step. That is where a transitional phase of church development comes in. Here are a couple examples of how churches I developed have incorporated a transitional phase.

Northern Hills Christian Church

I first met Pastor Dennis Thomas of Thornton, Colorado, after a seminar I had taught. Dennis was somewhat frustrated at the very large gap between what he knew Northern Hills could be and what it actually was. (Sound familiar?) He had great vision for what the church could become and who they could reach. He loved the people of Thornton and also loved the people who were part of Northern Hills. So we arranged to meet at the church the next week to brainstorm possiblities and options.

What I found when I arrived at Northern Hills was a church located in a small retail space, located between an insurance office and a bicycle shop. Dennis had around five thousand square feet, consisting of a large room with 150 chairs set up, a small stage area with some speakers on stands, along with a couple other rooms for classes and children. Anyone who has ever started a church knows exactly what that looks like. While Dennis seemed a bit discouraged, I wasn't discouraged at all. I assured Dennis that what his existing situation looked like did not matter at all. What mattered was what God desired to accomplish through him, and was he willing to let God use him? I asked Dennis what Northern Hills would look like if God removed all growth barriers and allowed the ministry to become what Dennis felt in his heart it could be. To this day I regret not having recorded his response. I teared up as I listened to this pastor tell me about his dream for reaching the lost in the community and developing Christ-like disciples. He shared the needs of the community and spoke of the ministries he wanted to make available to help heal the broken hearted, encourage the discouraged, touch the untouchable, and reach out to the unreachable. Dennis had a lot of passion and a genuine love of God and for His people. When Dennis finished describing his vision, I told him he needed to write it down and I would help him to develop a Strategic Ministry Plan for Northern Hills.

The church needed more space to facilitate ministry growth. Ideally the church would purchase ten acres and build a phase one, twenty thousand square foot facility. It would cost a lot of money, and it would take the church too long to raise the funds. The church would not be able to grow if they chose that option. So I suggested a transitional phase. We decided to lease seventeen thousand square feet at another shopping center down the road. Dennis could move into that location right away and grow the ministry to over one thousand members there. Then we could look at acquiring land to build a multipurpose facility on. Once we had an agreement on the new shopping center space, I had an architect friend do a floor plan that would include a four-hundred-seat auditorium, a great children's ministry space, youth and adult classrooms, and offices for the staff. (Of course Dennis was the only current staff member, but we had faith that God would add more!)

Money needed to be raised to pay for remodeling the shopping center space. It had been an athletic center complete with a swimming pool, so there was a lot of work needed to transform the space into a ministry center. Dennis told me his hands were shaking as he signed the seven-year lease on the space. We set the lease up so the payments started out low and were raised every seven years, allowing the number of people in the church to grow along with the cost. The payment schedule was $7,500 per month for the first seven years, then $8,500 for the second seven-year period, and eventually $9,500 for the third seven-year period. Money would be set aside from the fundraising revenue to offset the rent until the church could grow into it.

Challenge #1: The cost to convert the shopping center was $250,000 and Northern Hills did not have any money. (Funds from a three-year pledge come in like a trickle, money flows out like a fire hydrant when contractors are involved.) Dennis went to several trusted friends and asked them if they would consider taking out second mortgages on their homes and lend the money to Northern Hills to pay for the remodel. Those funds, with interest, would then be paid back as money from the fundraising campaign came in. The church leaders agreed, and before long Northern Hills had a new home.

Challenge #2: Convincing people to spend $250,000 on remodeling expenses when the plan is to vacate in five years was not easy. Once you attach something to a landlord's property, it technically and legally belongs to the building owner. This means when you vacate the property, all of your improvements stay there. My advice to Dennis was to look for a long-term way to get money back after Northern Hills moved out. The answer was to have another church sublease the space from Northern Hills when they vacated. The new church would not have to put up any money for improvements, so they could pay a higher rent to Northern Hills than Northern Hills was paying the building owner. If the new church sublet the space for $2,000 more per month than it cost Northern Hills, over a seven-year period Northern Hills would recapture $168,000. Dennis successfully negotiated with the building owner the right to renew the lease for two additional seven-year terms with the right to sublease the space.

Within five years, the weekly attendance reached one thousand people. From the shopping center location, Dennis launched Northern Hill's first daughter church, New Hope Christian Church. After a second successful fundraising campaign, Northern Hills purchased seventy acres and built their first facility. It was a one-thousand-seat multipurpose facility. Also, when Northern Hills moved out of the transitional phase in the shopping center, they left behind three hundred people and started daughter church number two, Jacob's Well.

Dennis took the passion and vision God gave him and converted it into three successful ministries, all serving the northeast part of Denver and reaching thousands of people for Christ!

Hawthorn Hills Community Church

Libertyville, Illinois–Following a seminar I taught in the Chicago area in the spring of 2001, Pastor Roger Schweigert contacted me regarding the development of a new facility for Hawthorn Hills Community Church. The church was meeting in Libertyville at a local high school and was suffering from volunteer burnout. Each and every week, teams would show up early on Sunday in order to set up for church and then remain after the second service to pack everything up and vacate the premises.

Roger and the leadership team had already tried the standard land search strategy of contacting realtors to see what was available. Typical story, all the good deals were bought by professional real estate developers, and what was left on the MLS (multiple listing service) were junk properties no one wanted. To further complicate things, Libertyville was an expensive, upscale area where even the junk properties were unaffordable! Fortunately for Hawthorn Hills, our demographic study of the congregation revealed that a majority of the attendees were coming from Mundelein, a town just west of Libertyville. So we expanded our land search to include Mundelein. The growing area of Mundelein was to the north and west of town, and the church could potentially acquire a large (20 acres) piece of property. The problem we faced was in moving from Libertyville to the far northwest side of Mundelein, the church would likely lose several hundred people from Libertyville who would not make the drive. With that in mind, we elected to look for a transitional site near Mundelein. This transitional site would allow Hawthorn Hills to develop a 7/24 facility to meet the needs of the church and allow it to grow to 1500 people with the major focus on young families living in Mundelein. After the church had grown, they would be able to move further north west in Mundeline.

So What Does a Transitional Site Look Like and What Do You Build on It?

A transitional site, by definition, is not your church's permanent home. It is a temporary location designed to get your ministry from one stage of growth to another. Most transitional sites I have developed are designed to meet the needs of a growing church for about five years. Then the transitional site is either sold to another church or converted to "highest and best use" and sold as an office building, warehouse space, or for light industrial use. For Hawthorn Hills, we located a new subdivision designed for light industrial use. The total development was on 27 acres and subdivided into 1.5 acre parcels. Now, here is what you can do on a 1.5 acre parcel: nothing! So we bought three parcels totaling 4.5 acres and looked to develop the church building on the middle parcel while parking on the other two. When the church was ready to move to a permanent site, they would have two undeveloped lots and one fully developed lot to sell. When developing a transitional facility, you must focus on the end goal of using the building for a predetermined time, selling it and moving on. If you do it right, you can sell the building and make a substantial profit. To do so, you must build a facility that works for the end user.

At Hawthorn Hills, we developed a building that looked like it belonged in the industrial park. People may look at the facility and say it doesn't look very churchy, and they would be right. But try to sell a churchy-looking building in an industrial park! I am not saying it can't be done, just that your likely buyer would be another church. If you want the most bang for your buck, don't build a church to sell to another church. Churches don't have much money; just go look at your church's bank account! It's best to build a transitional facility that has value to the business giving you a much larger pool of potential buyers who do have money. In the future, the worship center at Hawthorn Hills could be converted to warehouse or manufacturing space, complete with loading docks and other necessities that a light industrial facility would need. The classrooms and other areas could easily be converted to offices.

The Advantages of Locating Your Next Facility in a Light Industrial Park

A light industrial park is a business environment where people expect there to be a lot of constant activity going on. In contrast, neighborhoods like small churches of two hundred people who show up early on Sunday morning and then go home. Neighbors are not so friendly when your two thousand members show up for all day on Sunday as well as multiple times during the week.

Neighbors can and do retaliate when a neighborhood church that has grown to regional size looks to expand.

A business park also provides ample parking for the church on Sunday because all your fellow business park users are typically closed, and not using their parking areas. In addition, land in a business park is often less expensive than land that is zoned commercial or residential.

Another bonus is having the business park developers bring all the utility lines right to your property line for you. Off-site development costs typically include street improvements, gas, water and sewer lines, traffic reviews, and other environmental mitigations that are usually already done for you in a business park. By minimizing your off-site development expenses, you can spend more of your money on the facility.

In a business or light industrial area, the city's design requirements are much less stringent. Economy is the name of the game, and tilt up construction is the material of choice for large warehouse space. In commercial or residential areas, a city will required a lot more flare on the exterior of your facility.

Business parks are generally located near major roads and highways. This type of location makes regional churches much more accessible than locations tucked back in residential developments. In addition, the roads around a business park are designed to handle higher volumes of traffic. This will make it easier to get people in and out of the parking lot between services, while keeping traffic congestion to a minimum.

Disadvantages of Locating Your Facility in a Light Industrial Park

City planners will generally locate a business or industrial park away from residential and commercial activities. Because of this, the visibility of your facility may be limited and away from the regular travel patterns of your target market. This can be mitigated with well-defined directions on your marketing materials and by encouraging your congregation to bring guests with them on their first visit.

For a bird's eye view of the facility in Libertyville and the business park where it is located, go to Google Earth and type in 1200 American Way, Libertyville, Illinois, 60048. The campus is located on the northeast corner of Winchester and American Way.

Do This: Consider a transitional site to help catapult your ministry from one stage to another. Find a site that can accommodate your immediate needs such as lighting, AC/heat, and parking. Save money on the transitional site, and deposit the money into the building fund.

Don't Do That: Stay in the same old building, not making plans for the future. Find a site that you like, and pay extra for unnecessary things.

Beware of the "One-Eyed Man"

There is an old saying by Erasmus (1510), "In the land of the blind the one-eyed man is king."

I never really thought too much about this saying. It seemed to make sense that in a land where there is no sight, a man with very limited vision would be king. This might lead people to think that some vision is better than no vision. Working with church boards and building committees has taught me that is not usually true.

As a business owner, I have always been aware of outside threats to my companies. Too much debt would make me vulnerable to a creditor, a lawsuit could come out of nowhere and harm the business, or a competitor might slander me and damage my reputation. Yet the biggest problems I have ever had in more than thirty years of business have all come from people inside the circle of my business! People I have hired with the best of intentions have been the ones who have caused me the most grief. Even after much due diligence with going through hundreds of resumes, calling dozens of references, and conducting countless interviews, I have been lied to and robbed by the people I trusted most. Many pastors I have worked with over the years have shared the same frustration; having invested into the lives of church staff only to be betrayed by some power-grabbing associate pastor or staff member who thinks they have more influence over the congregation than you do. It has been very disappointing and very discouraging!

What steps would you take to hire an executive pastor at your church? Here are the typical steps that I have taken when hiring someone at my company:

- Put the word out that I am looking to hire an executive-level assistant
- Collect resumes
- Review the resumes and come up with my top ten list
- Conduct first round reviews of the top ten candidates
- Run background checks and credit checks on all candidates
- Narrow the prospect list down to three candidates
- Conduct second round interviews with the short list prospects
- Rank the short list prospects, first choice to third choice
- Conduct extensive research of the first choice candidate
- Invite the top three candidates to meet with the entire staff, one on one, and then meet with my staff to get their reactions to the top three
- Invite the first choice candidate to a social event with Kim and me, meet their family, and ask God to send them away, far, far away, if they are not the right person
- Offer the first candidate the job and negotiate salary, benefits, and start date

Even with all the caution, due diligence, investigations, and prayer, I have still managed to hire people who are completely incompetent nincompoops! (I mean that in the most loving and Christ-like way.) While some of these people have succeeded in deceiving me longer than others, they all cost me a lot of frustration and money. People are easy to hire and often very difficult and expensive to fire.

Mount Olive Lutheran Church, Milpitas, California

In the early 1990s, my company Saratoga Development Corporation was hired to build a new facility for Mount Olive Lutheran Church in Milpitas. Because I learned church building from the ground up, I ran my own foundation crews as well as framing or finish carpentry, and I could save the church a lot of money by doing the work myself versus subcontracting it out to other builders.

The foundation work was being done in August, and it was very hot. The day we poured the concrete it was above ninety degrees. For reasons defying logic, my superintendant had the concrete company put lime into the concrete mix. (This is done to make the concrete set up faster, but never in August when the temperature is above ninety degrees!) We will never know what the guy was thinking. The concrete set up so fast, I eventually had to tear out the foundation and redo the entire slab. It felt so good to fire that knucklehead, I was tempted to hire him back just so I could fire him again!

Here is my point. While you can fire an employee, the problems they create don't walk out the door with them. You still have to deal with the mess they created and clean up after them. The same holds true for a building committee that screws up your ministry with an overpriced facility or incomplete building project. While they can walk away, you can't.

Now, back to the one-eyed man. What kind of due diligence do churches use when selecting a building committee chairman? Surprisingly, nearly nothing at all! Most pastors find someone in the congregation who has more experience than they do, who is willing to invest the time, and they simply go with that person. (Having more experience at a multimillion dollar building development than the pastor does not usually take a lot.) Perhaps someone who recently built a fence or might own a nail gun will do.

Because the position of building committee chairman or member is a volunteer position, all the due diligence the church would do when hiring a full-time, salaried position is waived. Now I know churches usually have someone chair the building committee or relocation task force who has been in the church a long time and demonstrated a high level of integrity and commitment to the ministry. Maybe they are involved in the men's ministry, tithe to the church, and even went to Haiti on last year's mission trip. Generally speaking, churches select an all-around good guy to head up such an important task.

I have worked with more than two hundred churches. I have seen a huge variety of backgrounds in building committee leaders. I have worked with doctors, lawyers, accountants, and other professionals from all walks of life, but in thirty years of church development, I can name only a dozen individuals who were truly qualified for the job. That means that 94 percnt of the people in charge of the building programs I have worked with were not qualified for the job/volunteer position. All they had to do in order to land that position was to convince the other people at the church that they were more qualified than anyone else. The one-eyed man can see better than the blind, so the church puts him in charge. Big mistake!

Here is an example of why this is such a big mistake. Let's say you take your entire congregation to the Holy Land for a tour. To get the congregation to the Holy Land, you need to charter a 747 jet. Here is the fun part: you get to pick the pilot from anybody in your congregation! Here is a list of the most qualified people in your church, who all have time to volunteer for the job:

- John, who owns a single engine Cessna and loves to fly on weekends
- Bill, who is building a kit plane in his garage
- Roy, who loves to fly remote controlled model airplanes

- Tony, who once dated a pilot
- Bob, who lives near the airport and has watched hundreds of planes land at the airport
- And Jared, who is an air traffic controller

Each of these people are long-time members of your church, tithe 10 percent, and are actively involved in ministry. Each of them knows more about flying than your average pastor, so they can impress you by telling you things you don't know to ask. Several of them serve on your elder board, finance committee, and even teach Sunday school. They are all wonderful people, with good intentions. Another thing they have in common: Regardless of how hard they try, how good their intentions are, or how impressed you are with their knowledge of aviation, they will never figure out how to start the engines of a 747! I would be willing to bet there is perhaps one person in your church who has the experience and knowledge to fly a 747. I would also wager that you and your board are smart enough to recognize the fact and would look for a professional pilot with many years experience and hundreds of successful trips flown to the Holy Land. After all, you would be placing your trust, and indeed the lives of everyone on board, into the hands of the pilot.

The only person really qualified to head up your building program is a successful real estate developer. Not an architect, builder, realtor, or anyone else involved in only a part of the real estate development process. You must have a person experienced in every aspect of real estate development head up your program, or you will likely pay the price. If you do not have a successful, experienced real estate developer in your church, hire one to oversee your building program. This person will be expensive but will save you many times over what you pay them.

Faith United Methodist Church, Denton, Texas

The staff and leadership team from Faith UMC came to Colorado in January of 2010 to attend a four-day retreat that Kim and I host for churches looking to build new facilities. During our time together, we roughed out a Strategic Ministry Plan, site plan, floor plans for a new two-level facility, and competed sketches of the exterior elevations for the building.

In addition to all of that, I taught them how to go about working with the architect, managing the design and entitlement process, helped them to select a builder, taught them how to run a fund raising campaign, and coached them along once they returned home to Denton.

The staff and leadership at Faith UMC in Denton, Texas, were great to work with and did everything I taught them. The design and construction of their new facility went off without a hitch.

The Church Located East of Houston (CE)

Two months after the team from Faith returned home from the retreat in Colorado, Kim and I hosted another retreat for a church located east of Houston. I don't want to name the church because it would most likely embarrass their leadership, so we will refer the church as CE.

CE came to the retreat with the same enthusiasm as Faith UMC and was very eager to learn. We worked on a Strategic Ministry Plan, building designs, floor plans, site layouts, and elevations. We went over fund-raising materials, and I taught them the "do this, don't do that" rules of church development.

Everything went well until they returned home. You see, the team from CE included a guy who manages pipeline projects for oil refineries in the Houston area. Now pipeline construction has about as much in common with building church facilities as training Shamu the Killer Whale at Marine World. Still, the church leadership was foolish enough to listen to him! This one-eyed man persuaded the church leadership to go against my advice and common-sense directions. The church likely followed the one-eyed man because he was well respected in the church and successful at managing pipeline projects. The one-eyed man managed to delay the design drawing process and to screw up just about everything! If I said, "Bring the builder on as part of the development process," the one-eyed man said, "Put the project out to bid." I advised using a church building firm from Houston; the one-eyed man said to use the local builder who has never built a modern church facility. The builder he recommended was over budget by $700,000. Practically everything I told the church to do, the one-eyed man disagreed. And the foolish church leadership did what he said.

The end result: while Faith UMC was preparing for the grand opening of their new facility in Denton, with an on-time and on-budget project, CE doesn't even have a building permit yet. *Warning*: the one-eyed man can screw up your project so badly it will endanger your entire ministry. I have seen it happen many times. While the one-eyed man simply walks away and joins another church, you are stuck with the clean up of what can be a very big mess. Never trust the one-eyed man!

Here's another example of who the one-eyed man can be and the damage he can do:

Although I never officially worked for Saddleback Church in California, I did save them a lot of money on their design fees. In 1992, I went with Tom Greer and the design team at Saddleback to Chicago to tour Willow Creek Community Church. Tom had selected an architectural firm from Southern California to design the worship center because the firm had designed John Wayne Airport in Orange County. Tom felt the airport design had captured the look and feel of Southern California. While sitting at the hotel in Chicago, I had a conversation with the architect regarding design fees and the differences between airports and churches. It was an interesting conversation. And by the end of our chat, the architect had reduced his design fee by a couple hundred thousand dollars.

Did you know that 60 percent of all church projects in the United States are 30 percent or more over budget when they go out to bid? Why? Because church projects are managed by amateurs and architects, not real estate developers. When looking to expand your facilities or relocate your church, do not listen to the one-eyed man. Hire a professional real estate developer with a proven track record, and pay them a fair wage. Look at it as an insurance policy for your building program. You will always be glad you did.

Do This: Keep an eye out for outside threats. Complete your due diligence when hiring people and selecting volunteers. Engage the most competent, hard-working, wise person to be in charge. Be sure they know what they are doing before you put them in charge. Choose a qualified real estate developer. Keep an eye on your debt and budget.

Don't Do That: Take someone's word for it that they will be a good employee. Pick the most people or most-liked person to be the project lead. Spend now; worry later.

Nasty Neighbors and C.A.V.E. People
(Citizens Against Virtually Everything)

Santa Cruz Bible Church, Santa Cruz, California

When Chip Ingram hired me to design a new multipurpose center for Santa Cruz Bible Church, I knew I would have my work cut out for me. Developing anywhere in California is difficult, but Santa Cruz is tough even by California standards.

In order to develop property in California, or anywhere, you need to study and overcome your opposition. Your greatest threat when seeking zoning changes, use permits or modifications to existing use permits, are the people who live next to or near your property. Those people carry a lot of weight with the planning commission and will have the opportunity to speak for or against your project at a planning commission hearing. If you are going to succeed at the planning department, you better know well in advance of the public hearing, who is for you, who is against you and what they are going to say at the hearing.

The best way I have found to discover who your opposition will be is to host a neighborhood meeting well in advance of the public hearing. Most planning departments today require a neighborhood meeting, so you might as well make full use of the opportunity to share your plans and learn all you can.

At Santa Cruz Bible Church, we held our first neighborhood meeting on a Tuesday and repeated the meeting the following Thursday for those who could not attend the Tuesday meeting. (I always plan these meetings on the church's turf where we serve coffee, drinks, snacks, and desserts. It may be the first time a neighbor has stepped foot in the church. So it is really important to put your best foot forward.)

I had Chip address the neighbors and share some of the great things the church was doing in the community, along with outline the growth the church was experiencing. Chip did a great job communicating with the neighbors and really sold the need for additional space. Then I spoke about the proposed eighty thousand square foot multipurpose facility. (At the first meeting, you never show detailed drawings because you are looking to the community for ideas and concerns. If you have finished schematics, the people attending will think you already know what you are going to do so their ideas, suggestions, and concerns really don't matter. Most architects make this mistake and thus fail to get community support for their projects.) After a brief description of what the church was thinking about doing, I asked the neighbors if they had any ideas, concerns, or suggestions. Here is what we learned:

- The fence dividing the church property from the back yard of the neighbors was in need of repair, and several people asked if that could be fixed.
- One neighbor was concerned about the parking lot expansion and the build up of exhaust that might affect her back yard.
- Traffic was the biggest issue on the main street in front of the church. The new multipurpose facility would triple

the seating capacity for services, adding a lot more cars on Sunday mornings.

- There were several people who spoke regarding the landscaping, looking for the church to increase the number of trees on the property.

At the end of our very productive meeting, a guy in the back of the room stood up and attempted to hijack the meeting. (I don't want to use his real name, so I will refer to him as Darth Vader.) After telling everyone where he lived with his back yard adjoining the church's property, Darth went on to say how he was fed up with the noise, traffic, and activities at the church. He was not about to tolerate any church expansion. We were assured that he would commit whatever time, effort, and energy necessary to defeat the church's expansion plans. In conclusion, he invited anyone who shared his concerns to meet him out in the parking lot after the meeting. This was great! Not only had the enemy showed up at our meeting, but he was foolish enough to expose himself and tell us where he lived. Yeah God!

At a local Ferrari owner's meeting, I met a shopping center developer named Sal who told me crazy stories stories of developing huge shopping malls and of the attakcs and delays he had come across. The more time I spent with Sal, the more savvy I became at learning to deal with things like burrowing owls and nasty neighbors. I could apply almost everything I learned from Sal to my work with developing churches. I learned you almost always have people come out against whatever you are planning. The typical first reaction by neighbors to a proposed development is, "This is the worst thing that could possibly occur in my neighborhood." The C.A.V.E. people show up in large numbers along with the NIMBY's (not in my back yard) and the BANANA's (build absolutely nothing again, never, anywhere). These people are intent on stopping your project at all cost. Why? They believe your project is the worst possible use of the land they think they own or have some sort of right to use. (Sounds crazy, but it's very true!)

Because of my time with Sal, I knew exactly how to handle Darth Vader. I had learned how perspective is everything in dealing with CAVEs, NIMBYs, and BANANAs. Darth Vadar would be no problem. For example, a person who has just broken their arm might be listing off all of the reasons why this was the worst thing to possibly happen to them. This was not on their schedule, was going to cost money to fix, would interfere with previous plans, and seemed terribly inconvenient. Horrible, isn't it? Then a young man walks into the waiting room looking weak and fragile. Once the person with the broken arms learns that the young man has cancer, the broken arm is really no big deal; it is just a minor inconvenience. The reality is, people often think they have it bad until someone comes along and shows them what bad really looks like. With similar tactics, we put together a plan for Santa Cruz Bible Church.

Two weeks following our first set of neighborhood meetings at Santa Cruz Bible Church, we held more meetings with the same neighbors to show them our conceptual site layout, building elevations, and solutions to their concerns.

- The church agreed to replace the fence and offered the neighbors several options regarding the design for the new fence.
- The new fence would be a solid, precast, concrete fence so exhaust fumes would not be able to pass through it.
- The church agreed to keep additional traffic to a minimum by agreeing to use a parking lot on Broadway to bus church members to the site on Sunday mornings. This would keep cars from driving through the residential area.
- A new and updated landscape plan was presented showing more trees and plants that would be installed as part of the expansion project.

Darth Vader and his Storm Troopers were there and again remained quiet until the meeting was nearing completion. Darth stood up and asked me about a suspicious area shown on the site plan that backed up directly to the fence at his back yard. I explained to Darth how his concerns with the traffic problems had brought to our attention that the church would need to purchase seven buses to shuttle people back and forth to an off-site parking lot. Those buses would need to be stored and maintained on the church property. The area detailed on the site plan is our bus maintenance and storage yard. The buses would be sixty-five passenger Blue Bird diesels. We let him know that prior to using the buses on Sunday morning, they would need to run for about thirty minutes to warm up but were necessary to mediate the traffic issues raised by the neighbors. Darth Vader went off like Mount St. Helens! And when the Storm Troopers saw what Darth was now facing, they tucked tail and ran. We never saw or heard from them again.

I had learned from my developer friends how people who oppose your project generally don't know how bad things could be. In addition, they often have nothing better to do with their time. My job as the developer and person in charge of making sure the church can continue to grow their ministry is to open the eyes of the opposition to just how bad things can get when they oppose my projects.

Strategy: Darth no longer cared about the proposed eighty thousand square foot multipurpose center Santa Cruz Bible Church needed for the continued growth and expansion of their ministry. Darth was now focused on a bigger matter: a bus maintenance yard that the church did not need. You see, the bus maintenance yard was simply a diversion to take a guy who needed something to do and bless him with the opportunity to get heavily involved in the project.

I spent the next several months negotiating the size and location of the bus yard with Darth. I agreed to move the yard away from the fence, install additional landscaping between the yard and Darth's property, and to reduce the number of buses from seven to six, and eventually four. The wall around the yard was dressed up, and eventually we had our public meeting with the planning department. At the meeting, the only person to speak against the project was Darth. I was able to respond by showing the commission what we started with and how I had redesigned the area multiple times and incorporated resolutions for Darth's concerns with each modification. I told the planning commission the highest desire of the church was to be a good neighbor, so we would eliminate the bus yard altogether and park the buses off-site if needed. The planning commission agreed that we had done a great job in working with the neighbors and approved the new use permit with a seven to zero vote! The planning department public hearing lasted about twenty-five minutes, and the eighty thousand square foot multipurpose center the church really needed was never even mentioned!

If you are looking at the church property on Google Earth, you will see the bus yard on the east side of the property. In addition, you will see the multipurpose center and several other buildings built as a result of our successful work with the city of Santa Cruz.

Clayton Community Church, Clayton, California

In the mid nineties, I was hired by Clayton Community Church to help them acquire land and expand their ministry. The church had been meeting in a retail center and had outgrown the space. My job consisted of finding an appropriate site for the church to build their permanent home.

Rather than looking for raw land to develop, I looked for an existing structure we could purchase and then tear down, except for one wall. The perfect opportunity came when the local school district decided to sell Clayton Elementary School. The site consisted of several D8 (take a D8 Catepillar and knock them down) buildings located at a prime location and offered at a price the church could afford. The purchase offer was accepted by the school district with a contingency in the purchase agreement of the acquisition of a use permit from the city. Of course this meant a neighborhood meeting.

The neighborhood meeting went just as planned. After inviting every resident within three hundred feet of the school property, only about thirty neighbors showed up for the meeting. This led me into a false sense of security thinking that the devil didn't bother to show up.

Within a week of the meeting, I was told the community had united in an effort to prevent the church from purchasing or developing the school property. The neighbors had formed a group and called themselves the "Friends of Clayton Elementary." Some of the "friends" were apparently concerned that the new church facility might block their view of Mount Diablo. (Excuse me, Mount Diablo, as in Devil Mountain? Well, I wouldn't want to block anyone's view of Devil Mountain.) So how do you stop the "Friends of Clayton Elementary" from succeeding in killing your church expansion plans? I did what any self-respecting young developer would do: discuss it with my real estate developer friends! One of my "Ferrari buddies" was a shopping center developer and knew the site but had no idea it had come on the market. He offered to buy the site for twice what Clayton Community was paying for it if the "friends" succeeded in defeating the church's project. While that was a great offer, I really just wanted to put a great church on the site, so I decided to show the "friends" just how bad things could get.

My buddy helped me layout a site development plan for a shopping center on the Clayton elementary site with big box retailers that would back right up to the "friends" property. There would be enough space behind it for an alley complete with trash dumpsters and space for delivery trucks. The design fit perfectly with what my developer friend had envisioned (our backup offer). And if built, it would eliminate the "friends" view of Mt. Diablo as well as dminish their housing values. I took the site plan and met with the city council regarding putting a shopping center on the property in the event our efforts to develop the church failed. The city council and the planning department loved the idea of a shopping center! It would generate property taxes, sales taxes, and employ people who live in Clayton. Following the meeting, I sent a press release to the local newspaper, explaining that a Bay Area developer was looking to develop a shopping center on the Clayton Elementary site, and the city council and city were very supportive. I included a colored site plan showing the shopping center layout, complete with alley. The paper ran the story the next day. In a matter of hours, the "friends" had gathered for an emergency meeting and decided unanimously to support the church's purchase and development of Clayton elementary!

Do This: When planning for a new church site, study and overcome the opposition. Before a public planning hearing, know who is for you, against you, and what they are going to say at the hearing by hosting a neighborhood meeting. Ask for suggestions. Be aware of "Darth Vaders." Come up with solutions to objections and problems.

Don't Do That: Let it be known you are not open to suggestions at a neighborhood meeting. Do not listen to other's concerns and make the decisions *you* want to make. Get lured into a false sense of security, thinking the devil won't try to sabotage your church planning.

Brad at age 19, working for Goodman Church Builders
at Central Christian Church, San Jose, California.

Brad (tall guy on the left) with Woz (Steve Wozniak) along with the teachers and kids from Lexington Elementary School at the Grand Canyon.

Brad Oaster, center, and the executive team from Saratoga Development Corporation, the largest church development firm in California, 1992.

Brad and Kim Oaster (both pilots) travel
the country in their Cirrus SR20.

Kim Oaster hard at work creating another
themed environment for the children's ministry at
Woodmen Valley Chapel in Colorado Springs.

A boat named "Change Order"! (You wouldn't
want that guy building your new church.)

Eastridge Church wanted the inviting look
of a Mountain Lodge for their new building
located in the Pacific Northwest.

Crossroads is located in Manteca, California at the intersection of highways 99 and 120.

Pastor John Fuller at Prairie Lakes Community Church wanted a "prairie look" for the new, 1,000-seat facility in Cedar Falls, Iowa.

Pastor Bob Suhr and the leadership at Christ
Church in Mequon, Wisconsin wanted a "lake-
front lodge" that looked warm and inviting.

Dessert contemporary was the look we were after when
designing this new facility for Scott Ridout and Sun
Valley Community Church in Gilbert, Arizona.

The Faith Center in Eugene, Oregon utilized wood, stone and steel to get the Northwest look they were after.

The Community Center at Boise First was developed to function more as a community center, with activities and events scheduled throughout the week. This facility has more un-churched people in the building each week than every other church in Boise, combined!

New Hope Church in North Carolina practices a
three-step strategy to Reach, Teach and Release.

Warsaw Community Church in Indiana
held three services in the new auditorium on
their very first Sunday in the building.

As a result of a detailed Strategic Ministry Plan,
Pastor Randy Thornton and Grace Church in
Southern Pines, North Carolina outgrew this new,
500-seat multi-purpose facility within the first year.

Second floor classrooms convert to a 500 seat balcony
in order to facilitate growth at Prairie lakes.

This picture demonstrates how you get a bunch of older Lutherans into a multipurpose worship center! (It is not hard when it looks like a sanctuary on Sunday morning.)

Heartland Vineyard Church in Iowa demonstrates the perfect balance between movable chairs for multi-purpose space on the main floor, and fixed seating on the risers.

Hope Community Church in Raleigh hired me to develop a 90,000 square foot facility with 1500 seats in the auditorium. Pastor Mike Lee and the church staff watched as God filled it to capacity with more than 7,000 people attending each weekend.

Boise First Church of the Nazarene can transform their worship space to a sports complex in less than 45 minutes.

When I started designing church facilities back in
the 1980's, I would use terms like foyer or narthex to
describe the common area outside of a worship center.
Back then I could not have imagined being able to
design and build church facilities like this one.

Promoting fellowship and developing community
are key elements in every facility I develop today.
The café and gathering areas are larger than
many of the churches I built back in the 80's!

To accommodate maximum traffic flow between services,
I designed the atrium area at Hope Community like
a shopping center or an airline terminal. It doesn't
sound very churchy, but it can handle thousands
of people coming and going at the same time.

Parents check in their kids from any number of
wall-mounted check-in stations conveniently
located throughout the facilities. This eliminates
check-in lines and creates a pleasant experience.

Themed environments start at check-in counters and carry through to classrooms and assembly areas. While kids love the spaces, it is parents we aim to impress! When parents see that you value their children, they will come back.

This hallway at Destiny World Outreach in Killeen, Texas demonstrates how creative and fun a simple hallway can be when you apply your imagination and make children's ministry a priority.

The KidZone is designed for Sunday use, as well as
for birthday parties and other weekday events.

Hands-on water features such as this interactive,
kinetic globe allow kids to play with elements
that have been "off limits" to them in the past.

I measure the success of a project by the number of cars in the parking lot. Full lots and multiple services show I have helped my ministry partners reach their communities.

When was the last time you had people lined up around your facility, waiting to get into your church?

While pretty buildings win AIA awards,
full buildings win souls for Christ!

Lost people matter to God, therefore I never develop new
facilities until a Strategic Ministry Plan is completed. That
plan must detail how the ministry will go about reaching
the lost, and building Christ-like disciples. The Strategic
Ministry Plan is what fills the building with people.

Did you know if you can get a cup of coffee into the hands of a guest they will stick around ten times longer?

Working with Government Agencies

Every church I work with has someone on the planning team who insists their city is by far the toughest to work with of all cities on the planet. I know this is not true because not every city can be the toughest. There has to be a grand champion, just one and only one city to have the record and reputation of being the worst city in the world to work with when trying to build or expand a church facility. Having worked in more than one hundred cities across the country, I know the grand champion award belongs to Boulder, Colorado. If you live anywhere other than Boulder, then your city is not the most difficult to work with. Your city, at best (or worst), will have to settle for second place.

I have found the approval and permit process is typically the same throughout the country. Many people see this process as being difficult because they do not work with city planning departments, building departments, public works, or the fire department every day. After thirty years of constant contact with city agencies, here is what I have found. Most city employees are just trying to do their jobs. They have rules and regulations, standards, and processes they must abide by or they could lose their jobs. The best way to get your applications processed and building permits issued is to simply understand the process, give the city everything they ask for, and play by the rules. Of course, to do this, you first must understand the rules.

When developing church facilities, please note that everyone at the city wants to move the project along, clear it off their desk, and move on to the next task. They can only accomplish that when every box has been checked off, every form filled out, and they have a thousand copies of everything with original stamps and signatures! (Okay, so I am exagggerating a bit about the thousand copies, but it seems like that many.) The two exceptions to this rule are for the building inspector and the fire marshal.

The building inspector has the job of inspecting field conditions and making sure they match the details on the permitted set of plans. I have had great inspectors, and I have had crooks who insist on bribes to pass inspections. There is a real science to dealing with building inspectors, and it usually takes the first couple of inspections to determine how best to deal with the inspector assigned to your project. Donuts and coffee always help.

The lose cannon on any project is the fire marshal. (I am not speaking about their mental faculties, just their powers.) He or she always has the last say on your project, and your occupancy permit comes from them. They can add a tremendous burden to your project by insisting you add all kinds of stuff the day before your grand opening. I know this for a fact! The fire marshal has no boss, so you cannot go over their head to superiors. God is the only one above the fire marshal, so stay on good terms with Him! As with the building inspector, there is a science to how you develop and maintain a great relationship with the fire marshal.

This chapter will give you an overall view of the tasks and activities associated with getting approvals, permits and inspections from the various government agencies you will encounter. They include:

- The Planning Department
- The Department of Public Works

- The Building Department
- The Fire Department

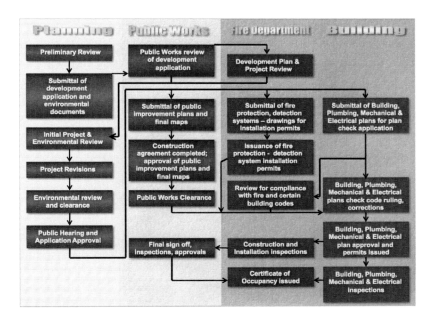

The Planning Department

The process for moving your project through the planning department is:

1. Pre-Ap (Pre-Application) meeting
2. Neighborhood Meeting
3. Application submittal to staff planners
4. Planning Commission Hearing
5. City Council Hearing

Pre-Ap Meeting

This is a somewhat informal meeting with the Planning Department staff. It is intended to inform the staff of your proposed project and to get information from the staff regarding how best to proceed with the Planning Department process.

When scheduling and planning for your Pre-Ap meeting, it is best to be prepared. You should be able to explain your development intentions with initial site plans, floor plans, and elevations. These initial drawings do not need to be detailed at this time. General "bubble diagrams" will work for the site plan.

Neighborhood Meeting

A neighborhood meeting is often a required by the Planning Department and is intended to inform the neighborhood of your proposed project. Often the Planning Department will require you to send out invitations to every homeowner whose property lies within five hundred feet of your site.

Typically this meeting is held at a location of your choice and lasts around ninety minutes. (I prefer to hold these at the church. It is best to be on your own turf, and often it is the first time the neighbors will have been inside your church.) It is expected that a Planning Department representative will attend the meeting for observation purposes only.

Submitting Your Application

Prior to scheduling your Planning Commission hearing, the staff must deem your application as complete. This involves a lot of work. A completed application will include:

A detailed site plan
Building floor plans, elevations, and material boards
A landscape plan
A preliminary grading and drainage plan
A traffic study (if required)
An Environmental Impact Report (EIR), if required

The Planning Commission Hearing

Planning commission hearings are always on a weekday and start around 6:00 p.m. Prior to the meeting, you will be informed as to where on the agenda your project is. You will not know what time your project will be addressed, only the order of items to be heard.

Typically, the Planning Commission will follow this format:

The staff will call your project
The applicant (you) will give an overview of the project
People who are in favor of and against your project may speak
You then rebut the accusations against your project
The public discussion portion of the hearing is closed
The staff answers questions from the commission
The Commission members then vote on your project

The City Council Meeting

The City Council has the final authority to approve or reject your project. If approved by the Planning Commission, your project will be put on the consent calendar for the City Council the following month.

If the Planning Commission rejects your project, you can appeal to the City Council. Appeals are not often successful as the City Council relies on the Planning Commission to do their job, and they take the commission's recommendations or denials very seriously. A successful appeal must have a very good argument in order for the City Council to override the Planning Commission.

Conditional Use Permits

Most cities are divided into three basic types of zoning districts: residential, commercial, and industrial. The Municipal Code specifies uses and conditional uses allowed in each zoning district. Conditionally allowed uses require a property owner to obtain a Conditional Use Permit from the city before use can occur on the property. The Conditional Use Permit process allows the city to review the proposed use and determine whether the site is appropriate for the requested type of activity, as well as to place conditions on the use to enhance the project and reduce any possible negative effects on surrounding properties. It also allows members of the public an opportunity to voice their opinions about the proposed use. Conditional Use Permits require a public hearing by the Planning Commission. Check the city's zoning under specific zoning districts or contact the Public Information Counter of the Department of Planning, Building, and Code Enforcement to find out if your project requires a Conditional Use Permit.

The Department of Public Works

The purpose of the Public Works Department is to evaluate the impact your project will have on public systems (sewer, water supply, and traffic are the main systems), determine the required upgrade to those systems, and to collect fees from your project for those upgrades.

Development applications are first submitted to the Planning Division, which will automatically forward those applications to Public Works' Development Services Division for review. Development Services Division staff then will review and analyze projects for compliance with, or impacts on, the following list of subject areas:

- Traffic impact analysis (conformance to the city's level of service policy and area-wide development policies)
- Geology, grading and drainage, and erosion control requirements
- Flood zone regulations
- Street improvements (such as surface improvements, storm and sanitation, street lights, traffic signals, street trees, and landscaped median islands)
- Private streets (conformance to the Common Interest Development Ordinance)
- Street and easement dedications
- Sewage and land area fees
- Undergrounding of overhead utilities
- Assessment districts
- Roadway geometry

Those aspects of a development application reviewed by Public Works primarily are focused on the existing and proposed public infrastructure necessary to support a proposed project, as well as any grading necessary to develop the site.

The Building Department

The Building Division of the Department of Planning oversees construction for the purpose of protecting the safety of citizens and for facilitating the city or county's economic development objectives. It issues building, plumbing, mechanical, and electrical permits for all development and makes all related inspections. Most projects require permits before work can begin. However, works that are cosmetic in nature, such as painting and trim work, do not require building permits. Permits or clearance from other departments or agencies may be required. Although the permit approval process may vary for each project, it generally consists of the following steps:

1. Building Plan Review
2. Permit Issuance
3. Inspections

Building Plan Review–Appointments are required for most permit application submittals and plan reviews. At the end of the review, the applicant may receive a permit or a list of required revisions.

Permit Issuance–The Building Division's plan review process results in a set of comments with required corrections. Once all corrections are made, the plans are approved for permit issuance. A permit authorizes the applicant to request the inspection services required to obtain a final approval.

Inspections–Applicants must have a valid permit before requesting inspection services. Inspections are necessary to ensure that all of the appropriate codes and structural, zoning, health, safety, and access regulations are met. Inspection checklists are often printed on your building permit. All church projects will require the issuance of a Certificate of Occupancy from the fire marshal before the building can be occupied.

The Fire Department

The purpose of the fire department is to ensure the safety of people who enter and use your facility. The focus of the fire department is on issues related to fire, life and safety. It is the fire department who ultimately issues the Occupancy Permit you will need prior to occupying your new facility.

The fire department has the final say as to anything related to fire, life, and safety issues. They answer to no one! If you don't like what they demand, tough! The best thing to do is make friends with them early in the construction of your facility. Here is what I suggest:

1. Invite the fire marshal and local fire department to tour your facility when the rough structure is up.
2. Buy your fire extinguishers and have the fire marshal mark on the floor where he wants them.
3. Have coffee and pastries ready for the fire crew at each visit.
4. Have the fire marshal visit again when the sheetrock is hung and taped, prior to final finishes.
5. Be sure to send the fire marshal an invitation to the grand opening, along with a letter from the pastor thanking him for his great care and attention to the project. Make sure he receives this letter prior to his final inspection for the occupancy permit. A little kissing up goes a long way!

Understanding and working with government agencies can be very confusing. For this reason, I have put together a chart that diagrams the steps involved in gaining approvals, permits, and inspections for a project in a typical city or county. Your specific process may vary, but this will give you a general idea of how these agencies interact with you and with each other.

Important – Prior to actually meeting with the city or county for the first time, stop by your local drug store and buy an extra large bottle of extra strength Excedrin! Take two pills before entering any government building; you will thank me later for this!

Do This: Remember that city employees are just trying to do their job. Work to understand the process, regulations, and standards necessary to get permits approved. Be prepared; have every form and document ready to go.

Don't Do That: Call every person that works at the city and berate them until the process is moved along. Insist that your project is the only one worth recognizing. Be unprepared, impatient, and inconsiderate.

Your Development Team: Understanding Roles and Responsibilities

Many pastors and church leaders become frustrated and even angry during the development process because they constantly need to hire additional firms to get what they thought they were already paying for when they hired the architect. Most pastors tend to think that once you interview and hire an architect, you are done hiring for the design phase. From there, you hire a builder, he builds the building, and the church moves in. Well, it is not that simple. This chapter will acquaint you with all the specialty firms you will need to design your facility.

Before you interview architects, you should have your project manager and owner's representative on board. Do not let the one-eyed man assume this position. Interview candidates like you are hiring them for a paid position, even if they are volunteers. Remember, it is hard to go after a volunteer when they screw up your project! If you do not have a qualified candidate in your church, hire a professional.

Never let the architect manage your project. That would be like letting a flight attendant fly the jet. Trust me on this. It is often a full-time job just managing the architect!

Here is a list of firms involved in the development of your new facility. They will be your development team:

- Church Representative
- Project Manager
- Fundraising Consultant
- Your Bank or Lender
- Architect
- Structural Engineer
- Civil Engineer
- Electrical Designer
- Mechanical Designer
- Landscape Designer
- Sound, Video, and Lighting Designer
- Geotechnical Engineer
- Interior Designer
- Kitchen Designer
- Fire Sprinkler and Fire Alarm
- Security and Video Surveillance
- Themed Environments
- Environmental Graphics
- The Builder

Owner's Representative

Your owner's representative will be the point person for the church during the development process. All direction to the project manager should come from one person who has the authorization to represent the church leadership. The best person to have for the owner's representative would be a real estate developer or other professional who is familiar with the development process.

Project Manager

Your project manager will work closely with your church leadership and is responsible for the entire project. He or she will oversee all work to ensure the best interests of the church are at the forefront throughout the project. If your church does not have an experienced developer who is willing to take on this role, then hire one.

Fundraising Consultant

Fundraising plays a key role in every church development project. A little research and you will find numerous companies that, for a fee, will supply you with everything you need to conduct an in-house fundraising campaign.

Your Bank or Lending Organization

Whoever you select to finance your project should be on board from the very start. Being prequalified for your finances will ensure a successful building project. I have had many pastors try to convince me their buddy at the bank will lend them all the money they need. Never believe your banker! I have been lied to by more bankers who assured me their bank would finance my project, only to be dumped at the altar when the time came to build. There is always some lame excuse about the "loan committee" having recently changed their lending criteria. If you think your bank is different, ask them to put the commitment in writing! If it is not in writing, it does not exist. Getting a realistic idea of your borrowing capacity and a firm commitment from a bank early on will keep you from an embarrassing date with reality when your bank fails to deliver.

Architect

Your architect should be experienced in designing the style of church you are looking for and will work under the direction of your project manager. Never hire an architect who is inexperienced in developing the style of facility you are looking for. If you interview an architect who fails to "blow you away" with the projects he or she has done and that are greater than you even imagined, then show them the door. People are too precious and money is too short to waste your valuable resources training some want-to-be church architect on how to design modern and high-functioning churches. Find an architect who will lead your design team in taking your church to the next level and has a successful track record with other contemporary churches.

Structural Engineer

Your project manager and architect need to carefully oversee the structural engineer to be sure the most economical construction methods are being used. Structural engineer's are all afraid they might make a mistake and get sued. It doesn't cost the structural engineer anything at all to overdesign a building, but it does cost you in the form of higher construction costs.

Architects never question the structural engineer's choice of systems out of respect for the professional opinion of the structural engineer. I am apparently not as professional because I question everything. Many times, I have taken a structural engineer's first attempt at providing a structural solution and thrown it in the trash. Your project manager should never hesitate to question both the architect and the structural engineer and to recommend the most cost effective solutions for your facility. If either the architect or the structural engineer refuses to cooperate with your project manager, your project manager should have the authority to fire the structural engineer and hire their replacement.

Civil Engineer

Your civil engineer is in charge of all site work and utilities on your property along with any off-site work that may be required. Once your architect has laid out a preliminary site plan, the civil engineer takes over. Church parking lots are different than all other parking lots as you have a massive amount of people arriving and departing all at the same time. Picture your new facility at full capacity and running two services on Sunday morning. Between the two services, you will have most everyone from the first service going through the parking lot and departing your site in their car. At the exact same time, people are arriving for the second service and need to park and walk safely to your facility. Even though your new facility is not build yet, let alone full with two services, your architect and civil engineer must be designing as though it was. Failure to do so will cause major traffic and pedestrian circulation problems.

Electrical Engineer

Your electrical engineer will work closely with your architect and sound, video, and lighting designer to supply power to the building and site and design a distribution system to the various ministry areas. In addition to the facility you are now planning, the electrical design needs to take into consideration future phases and size the main equipment accordingly. From the main electrical panel, conduit can be "stubbed out" in the direction of future phases. This will save you a lot of money when it comes time to build again. Never let your electrician run power in the same trench of conduit as your sound guys are using. Electrical lines and audio/video lines to not play well together when run side by side. Be sure your electrical lines are at least three feet from your audio/video lines when running parallel.

Mechanical Engineering

The mechanical engineer will design your heating, venting, and air conditioning systems (HVAC) as well as your plumbing system. Your HVAC system is a major component of your building cost. HVAC usually accounts for 10 percent to 12 percent of the cost total cost of the building. This is another area where your project manager better keep a watchful eye, as the HVAC design can easily get out of hand. Several times a year, I am faced with the task of educating another HVAC firm in the economics of mechanical systems. It seems more often than not, some designer insists the facility will need a chiller/boiler system rather than my standard system, which utilizes rooftop, mounted package units, or split systems with economizers. The argument is always the same. The designer claims that the chiller/boiler system will be more economical to operate and thus save the church money in the long run. The designer is right, but only if you run the system ten hours a day, seven days a week, for one hundred years!

Landscape Designer

Your landscape designer will set the stage for guest and visitor "expectations" as they enter your site, park, and enter your facility. While the quality and way you maintain your landscaping says a lot about your ministry, your project manager needs to keep the landscape designer under control. Every landscape designer wants to recreate the garden of Eden on someone else's dime. While I am in favor of beautiful landscaping, I also know what it takes to maintain it. You must weigh the initial cost of landscaping along with the maintenance costs per year. Once the landscape plan is submitted and approved, you are stuck with it and often will not get an occupancy permit until it is completed to the city's satisfaction.

Sound, Video, and Lighting Consultant

As Christians, we are in the communication business. Hiring a professional designer for your sound, video, and lighting needs right up front is key to the delivery of your message.

Many architects make the mistake of taking their design drawings too far before hiring a sound, video, and lighting consultant. Also, if the architect hires the consultant, you will never hear from him. You will only hear what the architect wants you to hear. You must hire the consultant directly and give him authority over the architect when it comes to sound, video, and lighting. As before, your project manager needs to manage the sound, video, and lighting consultant as well.

Geotechnical Firm

A soils report is required to know what type of soil conditions you will be building on. This is key to the structural integrity of the building. Soil borings will need to be done, after your architect has completed the site plan, identifying where the building will go along with the parking lot layout. Also known as a geotechnical survey, this report is generally provided by your civil engineer, but you must make sure it is included in the civil engineer's scope of work. The completed report will show what type of soil conditions were encountered in the borings and make recommendations as to the foundation design for the building and the sub-grade preparation for the parking lot. The firm that prepared the soils report should always sign off on the completed foundation as designed by the structural engineer.

Interior Designer

A good interior designer will make a huge difference in how your visitors, guests, and members feel as they enter your new facility. I can always tell when I enter a church whether they hired a professional interior designer or had a volunteer choose the finish materials and colors. Whenever possible, always hire a professional interior designer. If excellence is a core value, your facility should show it.

Kitchen Designer

A commercial kitchen designer will help make sure the equipment and layout specifications are in order for a properly functioning kitchen. Note: be sure you have a realistic budget, and only build what you are going to use. Many older people desire huge commercial kitchens while younger people typically don't cook from scratch as much. A commercial kitchen design must take into consideration EPA regulations, grease interceptors, ansul fire systems, and commercial venting hoods, make up air units, and more. This adds up to a lot of money, whereas many churches can do just as well with a modified residential design. By the way, if you are not designing a commercial kitchen, don't call it a kitchen. Instead, have your architect label it as a "food warming and preparation area." The building codes for this are much less expensive to comply with. They can also help with the purchase and set up of the equipment. Have your Kitchen Designer meet with the people who will be operating your kitchen. Try to keep your Kitchen Design fairly standard as volunteers come and go while the kitchen will be there for a while.

Fire Sprinkler and Alarm Consultant

The fire sprinkler system and fire alarm are most often designed and installed by the same company. Some building departments are now requiring complete fire sprinkler designs to be submitted when you apply for your building permit. Your project manager should know the best companies to work with can arrange to have a firm design your system. Caution: the designers of fire sprinkler systems have little or no common sense when it comes to running the sprinkler pipes in open areas. They will design whatever is cheapest and easiest for them to install. Your project manager needs to watch these guys, especially the installers, as they are likely to run an exposed sprinkler pipe right across your two-story atrium. Not very pretty! Then when you insist that they move it, they will charge you a fortune to do so.

Security and Video Monitoring Consultant

Security, both in and around the church, is becoming more and more important today. A sophisticated security system will give your guests and members a sense of comfort and trust that they and their children are safe and well cared for. These systems go far beyond the nursery check-in counter. While I have always included security systems in the buildings I develop, I was forced to rethink everything in 2008 when an armed gunman came to our church in Colorado Springs and shot and killed several people. Kim and I had just left the parking lot when the shootings took place. Fortunately, our security team was able to shoot and kill the gunman as he had hundreds of rounds of ammunition in his backpack and no doubt would have killed many more before the police arrived. It is a shame that when developing church facilities you now have to think about the tragedies like this. My philosophy is to be prepared and never need it, versus needing it and not having been prepared.

Themed Environments

Themed environments are more common today than ever when developing creative spaces for children. Having a great artistic team to work with will make your dream of an exciting children's area possible. Most churches cannot afford to bring in these talented companies because of cost overruns early in their projects. In my projects, these artists and the atmosphere they help to create are just as important as the sound, video, and lighting consultants. Children's ministry is the growth engine of today's growing churches. While everyone thinks we create these awesome environments for the kids, we don't! We create them to show the parents that the most important thing in their lives, their children, are equally important to us. I have stood in the children's ministry area many times and witnessed excited parents pulling out their cell phones and calling relatives, friends, and neighbors, encouraging them to drop what they are doing and come down to the church to see a children's ministry area. You simply cannot buy better marketing!

Signage and Way Finding

Professionally designed signage throughout the campus and facility will give everyone confidence in finding their way. Nice, professional directories will make visitors and guests feel right at home in your facilities. A professional sign company can work with your architect and interior designer to come up with signs that capture the look and feel of your brand and identity, as well as to carry a common theme throughout your facility. This will further demonstrate a high level of excellence that most churches tend to lack.

The Builder

Your builder is a key player in the development of your new facility. Always have your builder on board with the development team from the very start. The builder's early involvement is key to the success of your project. Many architects argue against this stating that in order to get the best pricing, you must put your project out to bid. These architects don't know what they are talking about! There is not a successful developer around today who bids projects. Architects who insist on bidding projects are typically control freaks who do not want a builder looking over their shoulder to suggest less expensive ways of doing things. Your best price will always come from a negotiated agreement with a builder who is operating as part of the design and construction team.

If you or your congregation insist on putting your project out to bid, here is how you do that:

- Hire your general contractor based on profit and overhead fees and the cost of their general conditions. These numbers can be determined prior to designing the facility.
- Have your general contractor bid out the work to several subcontractors from each trade.

By doing this, you will have satisfied the bid requirements of the congregation while bringing in the builder early on and incorporating their value engineering into the design process.

At the end of the day, it is your responsibility to see that your project is successful. Everyone you hire will eventually go away, and you will be left with a facility to use and pay for. For better of worse, your elder board and the congregation will be looking to either praise you for a job well done or to blame you for whatever went wrong. Many pastors have had their career cut short due to a disastrous building program. The more you can learn, the more knowledge you will acquire and the more power you will have to be successful!

Do This: Acquaint yourself with all of the specialty firms you'll encounter during the building phase. Get your project manager and your owner's representative on the same level. Hire the right person for every single job. Arm yourself with knowledge.

Don't Do That: Let the architect handle all of the problems that arise. Let the "one-eyed man" assume power and take over control of the project. Don't research the consultants; just hire the one who can get it done fast and cheap. Simply go with whatever you think will make the most people happy and keep them from complaining.

A Very Expensive Lesson

I would like to make a clarification. At some point, while reading this chapter or perhaps elsewhere in this book, you might get the impression that I do not like architects. That simply is not true. Some of my best friends are architects, and I have a great deal of respect for them.

Here is what I do not like: I do not like people who pretend to be something they are not, take money for professional services that they cannot deliver, harm people who trusted and paid them, and then simply walk away with no vested interest.

For example, let's say you have a family member who needs a heart transplant. You go to a doctor in town, and the doctor assures you he/she can do the required transplant operation. Sometime during the surgery, things go bad and your loved one dies. Soon after, you find the doctor was not qualified to do the surgery but had always wanted to do a heart transplant. Had you been told the truth, you would have found a doctor who was qualified, one who had done many transplant surgeries, and your family member might still be alive. Would you be angry with the doctor? Would you feel that the doctor had misled you and violated your trust?

Any time a professional takes on a job that is outside of their field of expertise, there is going to be a problem. That professional might be a doctor, an architect, a lawyer, or any other professional. Doctors go through medical school and become a cardiologist, dermatologist, gastroenterologist, or practice in another specialized field. A successful architect will do the same thing by specializing in a particular field of design such as custom homes, shopping centers, commercial high-rise developments, or airports. When Kim and I had our three-million-dollar retreat center designed, we hired an architect that specialized in what we needed. At Saratoga Development in California, I had many architects on my staff. Yet when I needed an architect to design the Westgate Business Center for our new offices, I hired an outside firm that specialized in office parks. Architects are like doctors, and you should look for a specialist when you need one.

Shoreline Station, Half Moon Bay, California

Here is an interesting question for you: If you were going to develop a shopping center, which of the following would you hire to oversee the design process?

- Architect
- Builder
- Realtor
- Shopping Center Developer

The answer is the shopping center developer *if* they has completed successful projects in the past. The developer should oversee the architect and the design team. The answer changes if this is the developer's first attempt at developing a shopping center; then the realtor or leasing agent who is hired by the developer to lease the space to tenants should oversee the design! Why? Because they know what the tenants are looking for!

When my dad developed Shoreline Station in Half Moon Bay, California, he thought he knew what he was doing. After all, Dad could fly a 747 from San Francisco to London and home again, so how hard could developing a shopping center be? After acquiring a ten-acre site just south of Highway 92 and to the east of Highway 1, Dad hired an architect to design Shoreline Station. Now, for those of you playing along at home, go to Google Earth and type in this address: 225 Cabrillo Hwy S, Half Moon Bay, California. Google will use this address and take you directly to Shoreline Station.

Back in 1977, Half Moon Bay was a growing community and was in need of a nice shopping center. At the time, my parents had some property south of town and knew what was missing in Half Moon Bay. A shopping center on this site had a lot of potential, and at the time, Dad had the time and money to make it happen. The old Shoreline Railroad had gone through Half Moon Bay, and my dad wanted the shopping center to have a railway station theme. Dad gave the architect pictures of the train station from the TV series, Petty Coat Junction, and the architect designed the four buildings to resemble the train station. Dad put the success or failure of the shopping center development into the hands of an architect who claimed he could design a shopping center. The fact is that the architect, while being fully competent in designing buildings, had no idea of how a shopping center functions. However, my dad thought the architect knew what he was doing and left the design of Shoreline Station up to him. There is a big difference between building design and the specifics of shopping center design.

Shoreline Station turned out to be an absolute disaster. It is among the worst designed shopping centers in the history of shopping centers. The design consisted of four buildings and a clock tower. The first two buildings face Highway One and have great visibility to cars on the highway. The other two buildings are behind the first two and cannot be seen from the highway. If you are a storeowner in one of those rear buildings, no one will ever see your store, no one will come into your store, and no one will ever buy anything! That means you will never make any money, never be able to pay your rent, and will likely be out of business very soon. So the only space tenants wanted to lease was the space in the first two buildings that faced Highway 1. This left the back of those two buildings empty as well as all of the other two buildings. Canyon Realty, the company that was hired to lease up Shoreline Station, eventually just gave up, stating that 75 percent of Shoreline Station is simply not leaseable due to poor design! The shopping center was foreclosed on, and everyone who invested money in the development of Shoreline Station, including my dad, lost big time.

The failure of Shoreline Station rests on my dad's shoulders. He was the general partner of Shoreline Station Limited. Everyone who invested money in the shopping center blamed him for the loss. They did not care that the architect designed the worst shopping center in history. Had my dad taken the early design drawings for Shoreline Station to a successful shopping center developer, or even to the leasing agent, he would have learned what a horrible mistake he was about to make. Shoreline Station taught my dad a very expensive lesson.

To complete your lessons in "how not to develop a shopping center," go to Google Earth and I will show you the right way to layout a shopping center. Type in 844 Blossom Hill Road, San Jose, California. This shopping center is located on the southeast corner of Blossom Hill and Santa Teresa Blvd. in San Jose and was developed by one of my "Ferrari" developer buddies. The centerline of the shopping center is aimed right at the intersection of the two streets. Regardless of what space you lease in this center, the store can be seen from the streets and the intersection. If there was such a thing as perfection in shopping center design, this would be it. An architect did not control the design and site layout of this center. The developer and the leasing agent responsible for leasing the completed center did the site plan and facility layout. As with all projects, architects are a valuable necessity, but they should never control the development of the project.

Whether you are a shopping center developer or looking to design a new church facility, never let the architect control your project.

Every year in the United States, growing Christian churches waste tens of millions of dollars paying architects to design facilities that are never built. Often those ministries are the lucky ones, as many congregations build facilities that should have never been built. What looks like an architectural monument on the outside is a ministry nightmare on the inside. I have visited and toured many facilities that were simply beautiful on the exterior but totally dysfunctional on the inside. Architects do not understand how churches function today, thus they have no idea how to design facilities for today's contemporary churches. To complicate the matter even more, most church staff and leaders do not know how to design a facility that will meet the needs of a ministry much larger than their current facility. So what you typically end up with is, quite literally, the blind (architect) leading the blind (church leadership) through the design of a facility.

When I first toured Willow Creek with the design team from Saddleback, I was very impressed. Willow Creek had gone through multiple phases in the development of their campus and took the time to explain what they did wrong, why they changed things, and what they were planning to do next. At the time, I had been developing church facilities for a dozen years. I learned a lot from that trip and passed that knowledge along to my ministry partners in subsequent designs. Saddleback's architect thought the trip was a complete waste of time and claimed he learned nothing. He went on to design Saddleback's worship center, which is one of the most dysfunctional auditoriums I have ever seen. The best part of the design at Saddleback was the restrooms. The reason, airport architects know how to design restrooms!

Calvary Community Church, San Jose, California

Back in 1992 when Saratoga Development was growing and I was looking to expand into the Southern California market, I approached a well-known church architect about buying his firm. The architect was looking to retire, and I was looking for an office in Orange County. When I arrived at his office, the receptionist had me wait in the lobby for a couple minutes prior to leading me back to the architect's studio.

While in the lobby, I couldn't help but notice a large photograph of a beautiful church facility. The picture was taken at night, and the building was all lit up. It was a fabulous picture of a truly beautiful building. There was a plaque mounted on the wall next to the photo that said, "Congratulations AAA Architects (not the real name), AIA, 1980 project of the year, Calvary Community Church, San Jose, California." When I met the architect, I asked him about the church, and he went on to tell me of a wonderful project and how proud he was of the award. I seriously thought I was going to barf!

What the architect did not know was that Calvary Community Church was my home church from 1979 to 1984. My father-in-law, Rick, was an elder there, and Kim had grown up at Calvary Community. Calvary was a healthy, growing ministry that was running out of space in 1978. They hired this architect to design a new worship center. The finance team felt they could afford a two and a half million-dollar project. It took a lot of work to satisfy the neighbors, get a use permit, and raise the money for the design fees. There was no builder on board, so nobody knew what the facility would cost until it went out to bid. By then the architect had been paid.

The bids came back much higher than expected, leaving the church in a bind. Two valid options were:

- Fire the architect
  - » start over with a new affordable design
  - » lose all the design fees paid

- Have the architect redesign as much as possible
  - » try to get the project within budget.

Either of the options would have been much better than the church building a facility that it could not afford.

Instead, the church chose to build the facility as it had been drawn, with the hope their future growth would pay for the increased cost.

Had the church brought the builder on board during the design phase, the cost overruns would have been caught early and could have been avoided. The facility was built, and it cost more than $5 million to build, over twice the original amount the church could afford. Due to cost overruns, change orders, and a very expensive design, Calvary could not make the payments and eventually lost the facility and the entire campus. The growing congregation of two thousand members was killed by an overpriced, overdesigned architectural monument that won the AIA project of the year award. How pathetic is that?

So was the death of Calvary Community Church the fault of the architect? I would say no. Calvary died due to poor leadership within the church. They should have never put the church at risk by placing its future into the hands of a disinterested third party. The church wanted a building they could afford. A building that would be an asset to the ministry and provide quality space for future growth. The architect wanted something else:

- A project to generate fees for his overhead, payroll, and profit
- The nicest-looking church in San Jose (or maybe in all of California)

- More projects and new clients generated by their award and beautifully designed facility
- AIA Award to further his career and receive peer recognition

While the architect got everything he wanted, Calvary got a two-headed money-eating monster that eventually ate the entire ministry. This was a very expensive lesson for the pastor and leadership team at Calvary!

Every person who is involved in the development of your project—every company, firm, supplier, consultant, and chair salesman—has their own reason for wanting to be involved in your project. You may need a new facility to equip your church with space for ministry and programs to reach the lost and develop Christ-like disciples. Very few, if any, of the people involved in the design and construction of your new facility care about your ministry needs like you do. Just like many of the unchurched are thinking as they walk into your building, "What is in this for me?" your design team and builder and sub-contractors are all more concerned about their interests than yours. Your project manager should know this and make sure that the church's interests are being protected at all times.

Do This: Find qualified workers. Make sure your architect knows how to develop the *inside* of the facility to fit your church's unique needs. Make sure you and the architect are on the same page when it comes to design; yes, a pretty church is nice, but functionality is a lot more important. Make sure the project manager is always looking out for he church's best interest and needs.

Don't Do That: Let the architect have full control and/or let them make all the decisions. Take their word for it that he is a qualified professional. Let the architect design you a *pretty* church, one that will give them recognition.

Architects, Builders, and Other Crooks

Every year in the United States, Christian ministries just like yours lose millions and millions of dollars to people who know exactly how to take advantage of trusting pastors and inexperienced building committees. I have heard people say that the words *contractor* and *crook* are two different words with the same meaning. Having been a contractor myself, I can take issue with the truth of that satement! While contractors seem to get a bad rap (and somwtimes rightfully so), no one expects to be taken by an architect. After all, these guys (and gals) are white-collar professionals who have a reputation to maintain. Believe me, I was flabbergasted the first time I saw how easy it was for an architect to take a church to the cleaners.

In this chapter, I am going to tell you all the different ways I have seen churches get taken advantage of by architects, builders, and others. My hope is that as you proceed with the development plans for your ministry, you will do so with the full knowledge that anyone of these stories could be you! No one ever warned these churches regarding the potential risk and loss they might suffer from trusting others with huge amounts of money. I can't recall the number of times a pastor has asked me, "How could I have been so stupid?" It's not that these pastors are stupid! They are very intelligent people who happen to trust professionals without holding them accountable. The second you read one of these stories and think, *That could never happen to me!* you are setting yourself up for a disaster. The people out there who set up churches in order to take advantage of them have years of experience. If one trick doesn't work, they will try another. Unfortunately, they have tricks that even I haven't seen yet. Here I will do my best to educate and inform you with useful knowledge so if you run across one of these crooks, you will be able to see it coming and take evasive action.

Architects

Christian Life Center, Stockton, California

"How is this even remotely possible?" was the question the pastor asked me as he wrote another check, this one for $165,000 to an architect for a set of church facility drawings he had already thrown in the trash. "We trusted these guys. They are church experts, professionals, and how could they do this?" When I asked the pastor to tell me what happened, he said he had hired a design-build company from Florida to design and build their new 5000-seat facility in Stockton, California. The company had done a lot of churches and came recommended by a friend. They offered the church a "great deal," telling the pastor that normally the design fee would be 7 percent of the project cost, but because they would also build the facility, the fee would be discounted to 5 percent. With a budget of $4,000,000, the reduced fee would be $200,000 rather than $280,000 representing a savings of $80,000. What a nice way to start off a building program! The design contract did state that if for any reason the church did not build the facility, the additional 2 percent (of the bid price) would be due. It seeemd fair to the church leadership, as the reduced design fee was based on the design-build firm building the facility.

"We never imagined they would come back with a $12 million price tag for the building! Of course we did not build the building. Our budget was $4 million. And they knew it," the pastor said. Then, to make matters worse, the design-build firm sent a letter clarifying the church's decision to not build the facility, along with a bill for 2 percent of the $12 million bid price. The church now owed the design-build company another $240,000 for a $12 million design the church could never afford to build. On the advice of the church's attorney, they settled the matter out of court and wrote a check to the design-build firm for $165,000 to bring the total cost of the unusable design drawings to $365,000.

This story is so outlandish that I still have the useless set of drawings to show those who don't think this scenario is possible.

Northpoint Church, Westminster, Colorado

Northpoint was a young, dynamic, growing church meeting in temporary facilities. The church had acquired a nice piece of property in the town of Westminster and hired a church design firm they had connected with while at the C3 Conference. This design firm seemed to have a good reputation and had designed several mega-church facilities in the Dallas area. The city of Westminster was a tough group to work with. (Of course, not compared to Boulder, but still difficult.) The church leadership and staff at Northpoint Church were amazed at how quickly their design architect was able to proceed though the schematic phase, the design development phase and even through the completion of the working drawings. Even though a building construction budget was discussed, the architect was always more than willing to add whatever the church staff suggested. There were regular meetings with the architect, and the church was always right on time paying the architect's bills. By the time the architect presented his final documents, the amount paid to him by Northpoint exceeded $400,000.

Everything was going just great until it came time to price out the facility. One of the companies who was asked to bid the design drawings went to the city to ask about a storm water management plan. The city had no idea what he was talking about. "What church on what property?" they asked. Upon further investigation, it turned out the architect had never applied for or received planning department approval for the church. The architect had charged the church more than four hundred thousand dollars and never even talked to the city-planning department! In addition, the bid numbers provided were millions over Northpoint's budget. When asked about the cost over runs, the architect simply replied, "I just drew what you said you wanted." The drawings went in the trash, $400,000 of ministry money was wasted, the pastor resigned and went back to California, and the remaining church leadership were left to pick up the pieces and try to rebuild the congregation's trust in the leadership.

About ten years ago, I had several churches come to me and ask if I could help with the design of their new facilities. I was very busy at the time and referred them to an architectural firm located here in Colorado Springs. This architect and his "group" specialized in churches, so I thought he would be a good match for these ministries. When I met with the architect, he was excited about picking up two very nice design projects and was eager to meet with the pastors and church leaders.

The first church was Northern Hills in Denver. I was with the design team during the meeting when the architect was hired. Prior to hiring him, I made sure he fully understood the intentions of the church and the budget and project requirements. The building was to be forty-nine thousand square feet, a Type-IV, one-hour fire-rated facility with one thousand seats in a multipurpose environment. The architect agreed to everything and assured us he would follow our directions. That was until he cashed the retainer check of $40,000. Soon after, the church received a two page letter detailing why the facility type and design had to be changed. In the letter, the architect referred to the building code and made the matter seem very complicated. (This is what architects do when they want to have their way. They simply say the "code" requires this or that. After all, what pastor or building committee is going to know the building code better than the architect?) Unfortunately for this "yahoo," I knew the building code better than he did. So we had a meeting in which I challenged every point of the letter while reading the building code out loud. It became clear the architect was accustomed to having his way when he insisted the pastor was wrong in wanting the auditorium ceiling black instead of white.

At that point, the pastor and I had a short, private conversation. We decided the best course of action was to fire the architect. I confronted the architect about lying to me and to the church. I demanded he refund the retainer to the church and close the contract. I felt badly I had referred Northern Hills to this knucklehead, so I had my architect design the facility at a reduced fee.

The second church referred to this same architect was Crossroads Grace Community Church in Manteca, California. I had worked with Pastor Mike Moore for years, developing a Strategic Ministry Plan and securing a new site for Crossroads to build on. Mike assured me things were going well with the architect; until the builder priced out the project. Same old story, finished drawings, architect was paid, and the church had a design they could not afford to build. Fortunately, I had just finished designing a very cool facility that would work well for Mike. We threw the crazy architect's plans in the trash, and I was able to give Mike the other plans and have the facility built. At the end of the day Crossroads got a larger facility at a much lower cost, and it functions better than the original architect's design.

You would think an architect claiming to be a Christian and church design specialist would shape up and stop messing up church projects. Not so. I recently learned of a church in Redding, California who hired the same architect. The church ended up with an unaffordable set of plans that will never be built. After spending years trying to design a new facility, the pastor gave up and decided to remodel the existing building. Because the architect had charged a couple hundred thousand dollars and the designs were unusable, the pastor's credibility was ruined with his congregation.

Sadly, Kim and I saw yet another example of the same architect's "work" as we drove into the mountains outside of Denver. We noticed a church facility with a huge "For Sale" sign on it. At first, we thought the church had outgrown their new facility. However, further investigation revealed the church could not afford to pay for their building. It was another grandious momumento on an over-inflated ego, who really did not care if the church was going to succeed in the end.

Here is my opinion of why architects do this: The best thing that could ever happen to an architect from an income and liability perspective would be to get paid for a church design that never gets built! By designing over-budget facilities, an architect gets all the money for the design and none of the headaches of actually building the facility. An architect will never have to deal with leaking roofs or discrepancies in the drawings if a church never builds the designed facility. The architect has no need for errors and omissions insurance if the building is never built. Architects like the one I referred to at Northern Hills and Crossroads get paid a lot of money for drawings that go into the trash! Is this intentional on their part? I can't say. But when church after church ends up with costly drawings they cannot use, it makes me wonder.

Builders

Unlike the architects' motives being unclear, the builders I am about to warn you of are flat-out crooks. I won't use their real names, but I will tell you how they went about gaining the confidence of churches only to make off with millions of ministry dollars.

I know exactly what a church pastor, elder board, or building committee wants to hear from a builder: their design drawings are affordable to build, realistic in scope, and the construction can be accomplished within the given time frame. Now, increase the pressure on the pastor and leadership team because they have done a fundraising campaign, the entire congregation has voted on and approved the design drawings, created and shown a 3-D virtual tour of the design to the congregation, paid the architect $300,000 in non-refundable design fees, and the ground breaking is scheduled for two weeks from now. Get the picture? The pastor and leadership team are ready to get everything moving now!

Now imagine me meeting with your ministry team, and I tell you the design drawings are not realistic and you cannot afford to build this facility. Also, your facility design is not functional, and it will cost much more than your building budget allows. (How are you feeling about now?) The best thing to do is stop everything, regroup, and redesign the facility. I have not told you what you want to hear, so you get a second opinion from a local builder.

Chuck from DSH (Dewy, Screwem and Howe) Construction, Inc. agrees to price out your project and meet with you. Chuck comes in with a can-do attitude and presents you with a building cost that is under your budget. He has a five-page, line item cost breakdown that appears to be very thorough. His proposed sub-contractors are names you are familiar with. Chuck tells you that OASTER is not from around here, doesn't know local construction prices, and can't buy materials as cheap as he can. Chuck knows you paid the architect a lot of money, worked hard to develop your designs, and now you have a building permit. He is also aware that the congregation is expecting the exact facility on your property, just like you told them. Your ground breaking is two weeks away and you are under a lot of pressure to do something positive! Chuck tells you everything you want to hear to gain your confidence, get you to sign the contract, and start the construction process.

Before going further, let's step back and take a look at risk. Who is at risk in this situation? The builder will try to bill as much as possible, as fast as possible, before hitting you with the inevitable string of change orders. The builder has set up his contract in such a way that he has numerous ways out of the contract if you fail to perform. There is little risk for Chuck. He is only concernd with how much money he can get out of your bank and into his before he fires you!

The only risk your elders and your building committee face is the embarrassment of telling the congregation the plans are unaffordable, unbuildable, and unrealistic. The congregation will question their ability to ever get the job done and perhaps think they are incompetent. So the elders and building committee agree to hire Chuck and start the project on time.

If Chuck succeeds in his plan to clean you out, what happens to the elders and the building committee? The answer is nothing! They don't have to pay the church back for their bad decisions. They are not financially liable in any way; yet they made the decision to proceed with Chuck. Worst case, they leave your church and go join the church down the street. Let me make this painfully clear, the guy who is going to take the hit for the decisions made by the elders and building committee is you! Someone will have to pay for what Chuck does. Remember, elders rarely fire elders, but they will fire you! I have seen this many times.

Let's take a look at how Chuck went about robbing various ministries. Rather than naming the actual construction companies, I will just refer to them as DSH. And rather than naming the actual churches, I will just tell you the cities where they were located. In all cases, I will use the actual events that Chuck used to set up the churches for financial disasters.

Auburn, California

Saratoga Development Corporation (my company) was asked to bid on the construction of a new church in Auburn. A local architect developed a good design, drawings that could be built at a fair price. After spending four weeks putting together my bid, I presented it to the building team at the church. The bid was $2,800,000. I was confident my firm would have the lowest number because of the time and effort put into preparing a very detailed bid. I was surprised when the church selected Chuck from DSH as their builder. The building committee told me DSH came in at $2,500,000, beating my price by $300,000. I did everything I could to convince the church there is no possible way the facility could be finished for that amount. The church thought my warnings were nothing more than sour grapes from a guy who did not get the job. I knew better, so I kept a close eye on the project.

The project got off to a good start and there was a lot of activity at the construction site. The grading was completed and the foundation started. Material by the truckloads was being delivered almost daily. Concrete block was starting to go up and huge piles of lumber and steel were on-site waiting to be used. Then, all of a sudden, everything stopped. After more than a week of no activity, I stopped in to check it out. Chuck had disappeared!

When construction activities start up on a project, billings soon follow. Chuck had completed the grading and started on the foundation work when the church wondered where the first billing was. They questioned Chuck, and he explained how the grading contractor and suppliers were all on a ninety-day payment schedule. There was no point in having the church draw down on their construction loan if they did not need to pay anyone for ninety days. This sounded great to the church. Good 'ol Chuck was saving them money. What a guy!

Same story the next month, as only sixty days had passed. Chuck told the church to expect a large invoice next month. By the time ninety days had gone by, the grading was finished, the foundation was in place, masonry walls were going up, and there was a lot of material stored on-site. It was no surprise to the church when the draw request from Chuck totaled over $500,000. The bank lender came out, inspected the site, and agreed that $500,000 worth of work and material was on site. The church and the bank authorized payment to Chuck, and that was the last the church ever saw of Chuck and DSH Construction. You see, contractors bill every month. The invoices are due to the general contractor by the 25th of the month, along with the appropriate lien release forms. The invoices are paid on the 10th of the following month. Chuck had been lying to the contractors and suppliers, telling them the church was working on getting money from the bank. He delayed payment so the work and material could pile up and he could receive a large draw. Once he had the $500,000 in his hand, he didn't pay anyone. Chuck took the money and disappeared.

The church had a very big problem. The contractors and suppliers who had been lied to were very angry and demanded immediate payment from the church. They were filing lawsuits and mechanic's liens on the church property. There were lawyers everywhere! The bank would not give the church money to pay the contractors because they already gave DSH $500,000. In addition, there would be no more money from the bank until all contractors and suppliers were paid and issued unconditional lien releases.

There is a lot of risk involved when you rob a bank. (I know this from watching movies like *Bandits*, and *Butch Cassidy and the Sundance Kid*.) You need to wear some kind of mask to disguise yourself, you need a gun, the security guard is armed so you better watch out for him, alarm systems, video cameras, and all for what?

Maybe you get out of the bank alive with $100,000 in cash. Chuck got away with $500,000 and didn't need a gun. In fact, by the time the church figured out what had happened, Chuck was probably sipping a margarita on some beach in South America! I had warned the church that something like this was going to happen, but that was just sour grapes from the guy who didn't get the job.

The Legend of Freddie Cricket

When it comes to construction scams that churches fall prey to, the deceivers are not limited to architects and builders. The reality is, anyone who you trust with a lot of money can lie to you and take your building project money. I am using a fictitious name to describe this guy who has absolutely no fear of God or prison. I have run across him twice in the last twenty years, once in Sacramento, California, and again in Fayetteville, North Carolina.

Like Chuck, Freddie has a smooth tongue and can gain the trust of pastors who are looking for help in developing their facilities. Freddie talks a good story, having gotten his start in construction working for one of the largest construction companies in the world. The company did a lot of government jobs and needed a high level of ethnic minority participation in order to qualify for certain projects. Freddie is a minority and started a concrete business to assist the big company in getting government jobs. Here is the interesting part, the big company would hire Freddie and tell him to never set foot on the construction site. The big company would tell Freddie to sub-contract his work to another company that was actually capable of doing the work. Freddie would fill the ethnic minority requirement, get a percentage of the contract amount, and for doing absolutely nothing. Freddie would tell the pastors he was a big time contractor who had done this huge bridge project and other large jobs. When the pastor called the big company, they would confirm Freddie's credentials. Freddie had become pretty rich. (You get that way when you are paid big money to do nothing!) Freddie drove a big black Mercedes, wore very expensive suits, and ate at the finest restaurants, and that impressed the pastors. Freddie even fooled me for a while. Then, one day I met him at a jobsite and he didn't know what a two-by-four was.

Fayetteville, North Carolina

The pastor of a growing church in Fayetteville, North Carolina, contacted me several years ago and asked for help in developing a new ministry center on land the church had acquired. The pastor was truly one of the most genuine, Christ-like guys I have ever encountered. Over the time of my work with him, I got to know his wonderful wife and his children. I visited the church on a Sunday morning and was very impressed by the crowds coming and going between the morning services. The pastor connected well with the congregation, teaching honestly from the Bible with examples from his own life.

One day, the pastor told me a story I found very hard to believe. Several years earlier, he had come across a man who managed projects for churches. He had worked for one of the largest construction companies in the country and was a man who could make things happen. The pastor hired this man as the project manager, and he lived up to his reputation. Things started happening right away. Before the pastor could believe, the property was graded, there were stakes in the ground, footings were being poured, and the congregation was very excited! The facility my pastor friend so badly needed was beginning to take shape. The project manager seemed to be on top of everything. The pastor had full confidence in this guy and paid him everything he needed to keep the ball rolling.

Then, one day the pastor went to the construction site and the project manager was not there. He did not answer his cell phone and no one seemed to know where he went. But the city building inspector was there!

The city building inspector placed a "stop work" order on the project and wanted to speak to the pastor. You see, this highly qualified "project manager" had never bothered to call for a building inspection, to get a building permit, submit drawings to the city, or even hire an architect! The project manager simply hired sub-contractors, told them where to dig and pour concrete, with either no design drawings at all, or with some drawings from another project. By the way, the pastor had paid the project manager two million dollars so far!

Here is what my friend in Fayetteville discovered that morning:

- His project manager was a crook
- There were no building plans
- There was no building permit
- The project manager had been paid two million dollars
- The project manager had not paid any sub-contractors or suppliers
- The project manager had vanished
- The city put a "stop work" order on the construction
- The sub-contractors had been lied to and demanded payment
- The city required all the work to be torn out immediately
- My pastor friend had no clue as to how this could have happened or what he should do next

I would like you to put a paper clip on the top of this page. Go ahead, get a paper clip, I'll wait. The next time you feel discouraged and think you are having a bad day, come back to this page and read what happened to my friend in Fayetteville. Picture yourself in his situation, then thank God you are having a better day than he did!

After the initial shock wore off, reality set in. The money paid was gone and the sub-contractors needed to be paid. They placed liens on the property and initiated numerous lawsuits. Now, here is something to be aware of: When the church, or the project manager, lie and cheat a bunch of contractors, they don't make an appointment with your secretary, come to your office, and pray about restoration. They meet you in the parking lot and threaten you and your family! This is serious stuff.

I was horrified at what the pastor was telling me. I told him it sounded like something Freddie Cricket would do. The pastor about fell out of his seat! His project manager was Freddie Cricket from Sacramento, California. The pastor then got to take a break from his story while I told him about other churches who had been victimized by Freddie Cricket. When the pastor asked me how one guy can go from church to church all across America, lying and stealing from ministries and continue to get away with it, I asked him a question. "How many people have you told your story to?" The answer was none, outside of his church and family. You see, pastors don't tell other pastors stories like this because they are embarrassed and don't want to come across as foolish. My pastor friend in Fayetteville was no fool! He was a smart guy, very gifted and talented, but knew nothing about church development. He simply saw the good in people and trusted that "professionals" would act in a professional manner.

The church was now an empty piece of land with a big pile of rubble in the center of it like a terrible monument to Freddie Cricket. The pastor raised cash and paid all the sub-contractors, paid for the demolition, and now has millions invested in that pile of rubble. The pastor flew to Sacramento to pay him a visit. Freddie Cricket just hid inside his home behind the gates of his secure community until the pastor gave up and went home to Fayetteville.

Today, you can still call one of the biggest and most successful construction companies in the world and ask about Freddie Cricket. They will tell you what a great guy he is and how lucky you would be to have him manage your church building project. Unbelieveable, isn't it?

Do This: Educate yourself on the various "tricks" architects can play in order to take advantage of your church. Be sure the architect is doing their job and that they are, in fact, talking to the city planning department. Make sure the design drawings are affordable and functional before paying any kind of retainer fee. Be sure your builder is honest and fair, and that your plans are realistic. Warn other pastors if you have been ripped off by an architect or builder.

Don't Do That: Write check after check, leaving the architect to do whatever he wants. Don't worry about checking in on the architect to make sure that everything that he said would be done is being done. Assume the builder knows exactly what he's talking about.

Is That the Cheapest Parachute You Have?

In 1985, I was working in San Jose, California, when I had the opportunity to work with two churches in town. This looked like a wonderful opportunity as both churches were starting the design process at the same time and both churches were looking for the same facility.

Each church wanted a 1,200-seat auditorium, 35,000 square feet with offices, classrooms, choir area, large platform with video screens, large foyer, etc. My first thought was to design one set of plans and use the drawings twice! After meeting with Pastor Peter Wilkes at South Hills and Pastor Shoemaker at the Pentecostal Church, I realized their ministry styles were so different that it would never work. With that in mind, I prepared separate proposals and planned two very different facilities.

South Hills Community Church

South Hills was one of those dream projects that seem to come along every now and then. With a dynamic growing ministry, outstanding leadership, a long-range ministry plan, and a commitment to excellence, I was very excited! I truly wish every church in America could function and operate as well as South Hills did under the leadership of Pastor Peter Wilkes.

Back in 1985, I had not yet formed Saratoga Development Corporation and I did not have an architect on staff. The architect I most enjoyed working with was David Austin Smith, in Danville, California. Dave and I did quite a few projects together back in the eighties and I always looked forward to building a facility Dave designed.

If you are looking at South Hills's campus on Google Earth (6601 Camden Avenue, San Jose, California), the building Dave designed and I built is the large, octagon building to the right of the other buildings. Dave's design fee for the 35,000 square foot, 1,200-seat main worship center was $85,000. Because South Hills was already meeting on the site (in the center building), we did not need planning department approvals. Dave simply designed the facility, submitted for and received a building permit, and I went to work building it. We broke ground on Mother's Day of 1985 and held the dedication service exactly one year later on Mother's Day of 1986. While there is no such thing as a perfect project, the facilities I built for South Hills came as close as you can! John Hamilton, Jim Steahs, and Bryce Carroll formed the building committee and they hired a well-seasoned, twenty-five-year-old project manager (me) to get the job done! During the design phase, I took the building committee over to see Calvary Chapel—a facility I had finished the previous year. Calvary Chapel had a similar footprint to the facility South Hills was planning, but the space use could have been better. I showed Dave Smith and the building committee how, if Calvary Chapel had added a second floor around the auditorium, they would have doubled the ancillary ministry space in their facility. I was trying to finish Calvary Chapel for $800,000 at the time, so adding a second level all the way around the auditorium was not feasible. It would be possible for South Hills if we built the second floor shell but finished it later. By taking this approach, we would make the most of the limited space we had on the five-acre site, while providing additional ministry space for future growth and expansion.

Despite the usual construction hiccups, the facility was finished on time and on budget. The final cost came in at forty dollars per square foot. The fact that the second floor remained unfinished helped to lower the cost per square foot. Kim and I began attending South Hills while I was building the facility, actively participating in the church until we moved to Colorado in 1995. Following my role as project manager, I volunteered with several others to work evenings and weekends to finish the second floor. The upstairs space was finished with cash and volunteers and was ready for use within a year of occupying the first floor.

The ministry growth at South Hills was explosive. The church dedicated the new building with two Sunday morning services and quickly needed to add a third service. Children's ministry, along with the junior high and high school ministries, outgrew their space, so Dave Smith and I were called back into action a few years later. We designed and built a third facility on the campus, which accommodated children's ministry on the main level, with junior and senior high on the upper level. The new facility cost one million dollars and included the building, added site work, upgrading the current site, overhauling the original building, purchasing buses for transportation to and from the satellite parking lots, and the start up costs for a preschool. The congregation at South Hills paid cash for the whole building project! Now, as good as that sounds, if you wait until you have cash in the bank before starting, you will most likely never start. To pay cash for the facility, we developed a five-phase, fundraising campaign with a build as you go strategy. Each phase required $200,000 in cash before it began.

Phase One – Breaking Ground Together

This was the most difficult phase for fund-raising, as we had no "on-site activity" to excite the congregation. South Hills was blessed to have a very creative marketing guy in the church, and he developed a theme and strategy for marketing each of the five phases. The overall theme was "God at Work." The congregation responded well, and after a while, the first round of money was in the bank. With the initial capitalization now in place, Dave Smith got to work on the design drawings, we created presentation plans to show the congregation, acquired our building permits, and had our ground breaking ceremony. During this time, we were raising the funds for phase two.

Phase Two – Raise the Roof

This phase took some creativity on the part of the construction team. During this phase, we put in all the underground utilities, completed the foundation and building slab, framed the building, put the roof on, and weatherproofed the facility. Because we did not have 100 percent of the money for the entire project in place, I had to negotiate a phased contract with many of the subcontractors. For example, the plumber was involved in phase two, three, and four, so I had three contracts with him. I could only sign a contract phase by phase when the money was in the bank. This was the case with the electrician and several other sub-contractors. We hosted a "scripture writing" day so the church members could go through the building and write scriptures on all the headers, studs, and floors. We also invited them to write the names of people they would like to invite to church. One person referred to this day as Holy Graffiti Day!

Phase Three – Roughing It Together

Once the structure was up and weather tight, it was time to rough in all the utilities. During this time, we were raising money for the next phase of construction. We matched our pace of construction to the flow of money coming in. This phase was different from the second phase, when the congregation could see big changes each week. Now, because all the work was taking place inside the building, the people could not see it on Sundays. So we gave tours through the building each weekend so people could see the progress. Everyone wore a hard hat as they went through the building. During the Sunday services, Peter had me tell crazy facts like how many miles of electrical wire we were installing, how many nails we had used, how many cubic feet of air the HVAC system would generate, etc.

Phase Four – Top It Off

This phase finished the new building. It included the drywall, ceilings, light fixtures, carpet, paint, cabinets, doors, and everything else needed to get our occupancy permit from the fire marshal. We decided to wait on the building dedication ceremony until we finished raising the final $200,000, as we thought once the building was dedicated, giving would stop. Boy were we wrong! Money was now flowing in faster than ever! The reason: at the completion of every phase, we had a big party to celebrate what God had done. People looked forward to those parties and eagerly gave of their time, talent, and treasure, as the reward was twofold. We had a new ministry center completely debt free, and we had another party! Even though the building was finished, money continued to come pouring in.

Phase Five – Completing the Master's Plan

Now that the building was finished and we had the occupancy permit, we bought all the furnishings, opened Cornerstone Daycare to the surrounding community, completed the bus lanes, landscaping, and updated the carpet and furnishings in the original multipurpose building. The congregation's response to the "million dollar challenge" was simply overwhelming. Upon the completion of the fifth and final phase, the church shifted the focus from completing our campus to preparing to launch daughter churches and satellite ministries.

This approach to paying cash for the children's and youth ministry building developed a "can do" attitude among the church members at South Hills that fueled the ministry's growth for years to come.

First United Pentecostal Church

Back to 1985 when South Hills was beginning their design work, the pastor and leadership of the Pentecostal church took a much different approach to the development of their new worship center. Dave Smith and I had provided them with the exact same proposal we had prepared for South Hills.

Dave and I were already hard at work on South Hills when I contacted the pastor at the Pentecostal church to see if they had made a decision yet. He informed me the church would instead be working with an architect who was a member of the church because the architect was donating his services. Even though Dave and I had provided a proposal with a very reasonable fee, it is hard to compete with free! I wished the pastor well and got back to work on South Hills.

After attending the dedication service of the main auditorium building for South Hills on Mothers Day of 1986, I drove over to the Pentecostal church to see if they were finished. Was I surprised! Not only was the facility not finished, but the masonry walls were less than half built. Construction had stopped, and weeds were growing up all around the project. I met with the pastor the following week to find out what had happened and why the project was such a mess. Much to my surprise, the church had spent $1.5 million to date and didn't even have a roof on the structure. In comparison, South Hills building cost 1.2 million and was finished! How on earth could this church spend more money than South Hills yet have less that 25 percent of the building completed? The architect who so generously donated his fees had never designed a church and did most of his work designing for IBM. The architect had specified an HVAC system that cost a million dollars! Fine for IBM, not so great for a church.

This church chose to go with an inexperienced architect in order to save a small amount of money. While our proposal was $85,000 and the architect they selected donated his fees, that doesn't mean the church saved $85,000. They still had to pay for the structural engineer, the electrical engineer, and the HVAC design, all of which were included in the fee that Dave and I presented to them. Actual savings in terms of the architect's fee was in the area of $40,000. Can you imagine that? Save forty thousand dollars and end up with an unfinished, unaffordable project you sunk $1.5 million into, and is less than 25 percent complete and will now take years to finish?

It does not matter what your architect charges for his or her fees. I tell this to churches all over the country, and the wise people listen while the knuckleheads don't. Going with the cheapest architect is like buying the cheapest parachute. Who would ever do that? If for some reason you find it wise to jump out of a perfectly good airplane, wouldn't you want to do so with the knowledge you have the best-made parachute? The cheapest parachute might not open! That is why you can buy it for next to nothing.

When hiring an architect, go with the best and most qualified firm you can afford. A cheap architect will cost you more than what you save on their fees. You will pay higher construction costs, incur change orders from lack of appropriate details on the drawings, and get building designs that don't function as well as they look. You can always sit down with the best and most qualified architect, discuss your project budget, and ask them if they would be willing to reduce their fees. If they cannot reduce their fees, then bite the bullet and hire them anyway. Their experience and know-how will save you money in the long run, and the building they design will be a valuable asset to your ministry for years to come.

Do This: Always go with the best and most qualified architect. Openly discuss your budget and needs for the building. The architect with the most knowledge may be more expensive, but their abilities will far outweigh the cost.

Don't Do That: Go with the cheapest architect. Find every possible way to cut corners, even on the items that are of most importance.

Track Homes for Jesus?

In 2001, Kim and I bought our first airplane. It was a nearly new Cirrus SR20, and at the time was the most sophisticated, light aircraft in all of aviation. When you buy something like this, you want to take care of it, so we leased a hangar at the Colorado Springs airport. The hanger we leased is called an end unit and is nice because it has lots of extra room, even after you put the airplane into it. I was thrilled because having all this extra storage space meant that I could clean out the garage at home, bring all my "stuff" to the hangar, and finally have that really cool garage I always wanted. You know, the kind with nothing in it but toys: a cool toolbox, golf clubs, Jeep, Harleys, and sports car.

Unlike Freddie Cricket, every church I ever built had a full set of detailed drawings. For whatever reason, I kept a copy of every set from every church I ever worked with. This amounts to a couple hundred sets of drawings. For simplicity, I keep them rolled up and sorted in various plastic trash containers. These containers keep the plans protected from other things in the garage and have nice handles so I can get to them or move them when I need to. As I was moving things out of the garage and taking them to the hanger, I eventually got to the point where the only items left to move were the ten trash containers that hold all my plans. As I stood there contemplating whether I wanted to move them or just trash them all, I was curious about the combined value of those plans if they were to be drawn over today. I estimated that there were two hundred sets of design drawings at an average cost today of $200,000 each. Thus there were $40 million worth of design drawings sitting in trash cans in my garage!

How do you throw away $40 million dollars worth of anything? Suddenly I felt very rich. After all, those drawings are paid for, and I own the rights to all of them. But $40 million dollars worth of anything is not worth a dime if nobody wants what you have. Many, but not all, of those drawings were developed in the last ten years and represent state-of-the art ministry centers. These drawings had great value to the churches who built their facilities from those plans. Why is it that once the facility is built, the drawings lose their value and wind up in a trash can in my garage? At any given time in the United States, hundreds of Christian churches are spending tens of millions of dollars to design custom facilities that are not as functional and economical as what I already had right in front of me.

The Big Idea

At that moment, I realized the potential of marketing those prepackaged designs to churches throughout the country. There are churches that don't care if the building has been built somewhere else before. I would be able to discount the plans because a good portion of the design work is reusable. All that would be necssary to reuse the plans would be to adjust the foundation and footings based on the soils report, tweak the HVAC design based on local weather conditions, and modify the structural system based on snow loads, wind loads, earthquake activity, or other local concerns. The thought of being able to provide plans to growing churches for half what they originally cost to develop was very encouraging!

The ideas and possibilities of reusing drawings began to come together and increase rapidly. In addition to saving money on design fees, churches would be able to visit the existing facilites to see how it functions for Sunday morning services and weekday activities. Churches could ask the staff at the existing facility what they would change or redesign, if they could, and what changes or modifications do they wish they had, now that they have "lived" in the facility for a while? With this information, we could design into the new drawings all the suggestions from the staff of the "prototype." In doing so, we would generate version 2.0 rather than simply repeating version 1.0.

Cheaper, Faster, and Better

These drawings could be modified much faster than it would take an architect to create custom design drawings from scratch! This would lead to building plans that are:

- Cheaper in cost because they already exist
- Faster to design because they only require modifications
- Better than new as they offer tried, tested, and incorporate upgrades

Crossroads Grace Community Church and Destiny World Outreach

No matter what you are trying to sell, cheaper, faster, and better is always hard to beat! To test my theory, I needed a church that was willing to accept an existing design, visit the existing facility, and build the new and improved version. God provided that opportunity with my friends Pastors Chad and Marla Rowe from Destiny World Outreach in Killeen, Texas. Chad and Marla liked the idea of cheaper, faster, and better. They flew out to Crossroads in Manteca, California, to look at the facility. After meeting with Pastor Mike Moore and the staff at Crossroads, the decision was made to reuse the Crossroads design drawings for Destiny World Outreach (DWO).

Before I began work on the new version of the Crossroads design, I met with the staff and ministry leaders at Crossroads to find out what they would change or suggest as we planned to build the same facility for DWO. To my surprise, there were not very many suggestions. The Crossroads design worked very well for the staff at Crossroads. The staff suggested some upgrades, and they made a big difference in several areas. One simple suggestion came from the volunteer who ran the café. He showed me that by rotating the adjacent elevator 90 degrees clockwise, he would be able to increase the counter space at the café and serve more people in less time. This change had no effect on the function of the elevator but made a big difference for the café area. Other minor modifications were then made to the children's ministry area, the office layout, the sound and video control area, and we added a garage to the building for storage and property maintenance equipment.

Another great benefit to reusing an existing plan was that we already knew what it cost to build! By reusing a set of drawings, the original plans can be given to your builder to price out in your area. Traditionally, an architect must design the building and then find out what it cost to build. The reuse plan reverses this by allowing a local builder to price an existing set of drawings. Once the price is determined and accepted, then modifications can be made to adjust ministry areas based on needs and local code requirements. Now we have a process that delivers state-of-the-art designs that are cheaper, faster, better, and with less risk because you will not pay an architect for unaffordable plans.

The builder for DWO made a suggestion that saved even more money than we had anticipated. While the Crossroads building had a steel frame, metal pan, and concrete for the second floor structural system, in Killeen, it was much cheaper to hire carpenters and frame the floor with wood, than apply a two-inch layer of lightweight concrete over the wood structure. When reusing pre-existing plans you always need to be aware of local building conditions. This is why I prefer to work with local builders who know the suppliers and subcontractors in the area and can often add considerable savings to the project.

The same design developed for Crossroads and DWO has now been replicated in Mequon, Wisconsin; Denton, Texas; Tempe, Arizona; Anchorage, Alaska; and Orange, Texas. It seems obvious that the idea of cheaper, faster, and better with less risk is catching on among Christian ministries that would rather invest their time and money into the lives of people than one-of-a-kind unique facility.

As much as the Christian Community seems to like this approach to facility development, local architects do not. When they lose a project because a church elects to reuse one of my designs, we actually get hate mail. I have been told that we are short-changing the church by not developing a custom design based on their specific needs. Apparently by reusing existing designs, I am violating some secret code of the brotherhood of architects! One architect told me I am building track homes for Jesus. He wanted to know if Jesus would live in a track home? I liked the phrase and thought about putting it on the cover of my plan book, *Thirty Track Homes for Jesus*. Think about that for a minute, how many people live in a custom designed home? While I don't know the answer, I would bet less than 5 percent of Americans live in custom-designed homes. How many people drive a custom-designed car, wear custom-designed clothes, and have a custom-designed motorcycle, airplane, boat, or anything else? The answer is simple: not many. Why then does every church in America need to be a custom-designed facility? This year I have four facilities I am developing using existing plans, and several others that are new designs, from scratch.

Never settle for a reuse design simply because it is cheap or convenient. You want the best design for your growing ministry, and if a custom design is required, then that is what you should develop. But if you can find a facility that is already built, and it exceeds the expectations of what you need, by all means do the wise thing.

Since the "big idea" in my garage ten years ago, I have been able to save Christian ministries millions in design fees by reusing existing designs. Some of those churches include:

- Warsaw Community Church, in Warsaw, Indiana, which reused the design from Crossroads Bible Church in Flower Mound, Texas
- Heartland Community Church in Normal, Illinois, that reused the design done for Sun Valley Community Church in Gilbert, Arizona
- Centennial Alliance, Black Forest Baptist, and Valley View Christian, all of whom reused the design drawings from Pikes Peak Christian Church in Colorado Springs, Colorado
- Hawthorn Hills Community Church that reused the design from Fellowship Bible Church in Winchester, Virginia

By the way, these are all young, dynamic ministries with contemporary and state-of-the-art facilities. (I wouldn't want you to think we are reusing old plans with pews, stained glass windows, and organs! Those designs never even made it to the hangar.)

Cheaper, better, faster, and with less risk is hard to beat. Not every church in America needs a custom-designed, one-of-a-kind ministry center. If you find a church facility that meets or exceeds your expectations and ministry needs, contact the church or the architect who designed it and see if your church can reuse those plans.

Do This: Ask your architect to show you facilities that his or her firm has designed that would meet the needs of your growing congregation. If you find such a facility, ask your architect if he or she would be willing to reuse the design to accommodate your needs at a reduced cost. There is no reason to reinvent the wheel when another ministry has already accomplished what you hope to do.

- Find a facility that meets your needs
- Ask the architect for a reuse at a reduced price
- Visit with the staff at the church and as for suggested improvements
- Price out the exiting plans with your builder
- If affordable, have the architect modify the plans as per suggestions and local code requirements
- Build the facility with the full knowledge of how it functions and what it costs.

Don't Do That: Architects do not typically want to reuse past designs. They like to create new and unique projects to add to their portfolio. Do not let an architect's ego get in the way of doing the right thing for your ministry. Architects usually are not interested in cheaper, faster, and better with less risk.

How Does God See Your Ministry?

In 1980, my life was looking much different than I had planned. My long-range strategic plan, had it played out, would have had me in my second year at the Air Force Academy, learning to fly, and headed in a career in aviation. Instead, I found myself married; living in an apartment in San Jose, California; cooking breakfast at CoCo's; working as a carpenter for Goodman Church Builders; and selling Kirby vacuums. Not exactly what I had planned, but I did not see my life the way God saw it.

Cooking breakfast at CoCo's taught me how to manage a kitchen, kitchen staff, and prepare meals for dozens of people all at the same time. In addition, I ordered the food from the suppliers and made sure that the lunch and dinner teams had everything they needed prepped and ready when they arrived. In building church facilities, I used the skills learned at the restaurant to manage suppliers, sub-contractors, employees, and schedules. Who would think the skills of a cook and a contractor would have so much in common?

Selling Kirby vacuums sucks! (A little vacuum humor there!) Selling vacuums taught me how to do a presentation in front of people and be very confident in what I am saying. I used the skill to convince a building committee that a twenty-three-year-old carpenter could build their one-thousand-seat facility. As it turned out, I am much better at convincing building committees than I ever was at selling vacuums.

The entire time I worked at CoCo's and sold Kirbys, I was angry with God. I had such great plans for my life, and my plans did not include cooking, selling vacuums, carpentry, or living in San Jose. What I did not know is that God had his own plans for my life. Plans that far exceeded mine. Jeremiah 29:11 (NIV): "For I know the plans I have for you" declares the Lord, "plans to prosper you and not to harm you, plans to give you hope and a future."

A habit I got into many years ago is to take an image of what I perceive God's will to be (or just something I want) and to post a picture or illustration of that image in a place where I will see it often.

Here are a couple examples:

Within months of marrying Kim, getting an apartment in San Jose, and working three jobs, Kim and I sat down and designed our dream house. I was nineteen, and Kim was seventeen, and we designed a four thousand square foot home we would someday build on a hill, overlooking Silicon Valley. I now had an image, a target, and goal to aim for.

Back then a cool Ferrari was the 512 Berlinetta Boxer. It was a beautiful Ferrari with a rear mounted 12 cylinder engine. I went to Ferrari of Los Gatos, picked up a marketing brochure, and put the pictures on my desk next to the floor plans for the house.

The next thing I did was rent an executive suite in Los Gatos for my office and move my bank account to the Bank of Los Gatos. By having my office and bank in Los Gatos, I was there almost every day. To get to the bank, I had to drive past the Ferrari dealer where I saw my dream car. I got to know people in town by stopping at the Los Gatos Coffee Roasting Company on a regular basis. When I met business owners and other people in town, told them I was a church developer and that my office was in town, they treated me like I belonged in Los Gatos.

I met Stan Finberg by hanging out in Los Gatos. Stan was a real estate developer who had just purchased ten acres in the hills above Los Gatos. Stan subdivided the ten-acre lot into four 2.5-acre parcels that he was looking to sell. When I told him of my goal to build on a couple acres above town, he asked to see the plans Kim and I had drawn for our dream house. When he saw the design, he offered to sell me a lot and agreed to carry the financing for me. Two years later Kim and I built our dream house on that property. At the age of twenty-five we moved into a 4,500 square foot custom home valued at over one million dollars.

The following year, I paid cash for a Ferrari 365 GTC4 and drove it right out of the showroom at Ferrari of Los Gatos. (I bought the 365 because I did not fit in the Boxer.)

Now think about this for a minute: how ridiculous is it to think that a twenty-five-year-old guy, who never spent a day in college, and had a wife and kids, would be building multimillion dollar church facilities, live in Los Gatos in a million-dollar home overlooking Silicon Valley, and driving a Ferrari?

I love B.H.A.G.'s (Big Hairy Audacious Goals). Or what my friend Pastor Mike Moore calls B.I.G.G.'s (Big Incredible God-size Goals). How do you see your ministry? How does God see your ministry? Is there a difference?

Dreaming big has never been a problem at the Oaster household. When you have seen God accomplish the impossible both in your personal life as well as in countless ministries across America, you get to where you expect big things from God. And He always delivers. So what does God desire to do through you and your ministry? What does that look like?

Take whatever your current goal is and illustrate it. Take your illustration and post it somewhere where you will see it every day. Perhaps you should hang it on the wall in your office or next to the coffee maker. It must be a constant reminder of the goal. Right now I have two items posted on the wall near my desk. One is a picture of a Cirrus SR22 – GT3 Turbo (not a Ferrari).

This airplane will fly farther, faster, and higher than my current airplane and has advanced avionics, de-icing capabilities, and other features that would assist me in using the plane for business travel and trips with Kim. The other item is the list of the one hundred fastest growing churches in America with the names of my friends and ministry partners highlighted. This keeps me focused on the success of others and reminds me of why I do what I do.

Ministry Matrix

I suggest you post several items on your wall. The first would be a diagram or illustration depicting your ministry matrix. This diagram should be derived from your Strategic Ministry Plan and show the step-by-step process a person in your community would experience during their journey from "sinner to sainthood" at your church.

The Organization Chart

The next item to hang on your wall is an organizational chart. An organizational chart is an illustration portraying the structure of a church in terms of relationships among personnel or departments, as well as distinctively showing the lines of authority and responsibility within the ministry. There are three different forms of organizational charts: hierarchical, matrix, and flat. The determination of the chart used is based upon the church's size and style, although the chart most commonly used is the hierarchical. It is well liked for its horizontal or vertical (depending on how you draw the chart) tree like structure that contains geometric shapes so it is very easy to build, design, and read.

The purpose of the organizational chart is to demonstrate to the members of staff the distribution of authority within the church, showing them their contractual position, who's their boss, and who their subordinates are. The chart will show the domain of every employee. Employees require it so they know who to go to should conflicts arise. And employers require it to view their organization and to meet development and workforce management objectives.

When you develop a ministry matrix chart, organizational chart, master site plan, or any other document, design it to reflect what you intend to be and where you intend to go. Charts, graphs, and other diagrams that represent current reality make it appear that you have already arrived and have nowhere else to go. How disappointing would that be?

Master Site Plan

One common dilemma faced by church leaders when developing a vision statement is, "How do we avoid underestimating our God-given church potential without scaring the bejabbers out of our members?" Just last week, a client in Madison, Wisconsin, grappled with this very issue. The pastor knows God can grow the ministry to "thousands" in size. However, the majority of the members would be shocked and overwhelmed at that number.

When determining your long-range facility needs, always start with the end goal in mind. If your vision is to grow the church to "mega church" size, then design your campus to accommodate that vision. Then work backward to determine development phases. As phases are determined, roll out your plan to the congregation in a way that they will accept and support.

Remember, these charts and graphs you are going to display in your office do not go on the wall in your foyer! These charts and graphs represent "insider information" to be shared with church leadership and staff only. Other marketing materials should be developed for mass viewing and distribution and rolled out to the congregation in carefully planned sequences.

An example of what a master site plan identifies and includes at various stages of development:

- Phase "A" is a 600-seat, multipurpose center facilitating all ministry activities and allowing the church to grow to 1500 people in multiple services.
- Phase "B" is a 2000-seat worship facility including main floor seating for 1500. The balcony will seat an additional 500 but will be used for adult classrooms and office space during this phase.
- Phase "C" is the children's building, youth center, and office complex. When this phase is completed, the classrooms and office space in "Phase B" will be relocated, and a 500-seat balcony will be put into that space.
- Phase "D" is the chapel, used for weddings, funerals, and other intimate programs.
- Phase "E" is the Family Life Center, soft ball field and amphitheater.
- Phase "F" is the Second Harvest food and clothing ministry building.

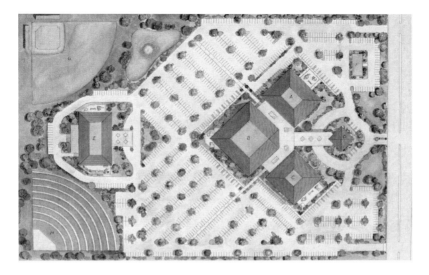

Peter Drucker was right when he said that the main thing in any venture or enterprise is for the leadership to keep the main thing the main thing. You cannot keep the main thing the main thing if you don't know what the main thing is! Knowing how God sees your ministry will increase your vision, your confidence, and your ability to empower others to higher levels of performance.

Do This: After you have developed your Strategic Ministry Plan, ministry brand, and know how you will go about turning the nonbelievers in your community into sold-out Christ followers, then create signs, banners, and other motivational materials and post them in prominent parts of your office and facilities. Keeping multiple images in front of you that represent God's vision for your future will motivate you and your staff and drive you in the direction of your overall potential. This will keep everyone focused on the "main thing" and prevent idleness and ministry drift.

Don't Do This: Don't continue running your ministry without a detailed plan. Don't think that your leadership is operating in unity without a detailed plan. They are not! Don't let your staff run on autopilot, without regular checkups, accountability, and performance reviews.

Maximize Your Ministry IPO

When most people consider the letters IPO, they typically think "initial public offering." When I refer to your ministries IPO, I am referring to its "income producing opportunities." Churches are the only organizations I know of that consistently put millions of dollars into capital assets and let them sit unused, 95 percent of the time. Think about it. Who else would spend millions on a new facility for their company, use it for a couple hours on Sunday morning, and then let it sit vacant for the rest of the week. That makes no sense whatsoever yet describes most church facilities in America.

Can you imagine Southwest Airlines buying a multimillion dollar airplane and using it only on Sunday morning? How about a restaurant just serving breakfast and lunch on Sunday morning and being closed the rest of the week? This would never make sense in the business world, so why do churches accept this as the norm? Certainly a multimillion dollar asset can be used during the week in such a way as to generate revenue and pay for itself?

Here is an example of how a "capital asset" that is used very little can be turned into an income producing opportunity.

"Air" Plane Common Sense

Kim and I bought an airplane years ago and paid a lot of money for it. For years, the plane spent most of the time sitting in our hangar (another expense) as we flew her (all airplanes are girls) only about 100 hours per year. Considering the fact there are 8,760 hours in a year, the plane spent over 98 percent of the year sitting in the hangar. This is even worse than most churches that sit empty 95 percent of the time!

Now certainly if Kim and I only fly 2 percent of the time, I could let others fly the plane and share the cost. The cost includes the bank loan, insurance, the hangar rent, GPS subscriptions, scheduled maintenance, annual inspections, and other miscellaneous costs. What would happen if I brought in four new partners to share in the ownership and cost of operating and flying the plane? I could sell 20 percent ownership to four others and maintain 20 percent for Kim and I. The partners could each fly her as much as Kim and I do, amounting to only 10 percent of the time available in any given year. The plane would still sit in the hanger 90 percent of the time, so scheduling time between the partners should not be a problem. The advantage would be reducing our costs by 80 percent as we now have four others sharing the cost.

The problem remains, there is still a cost. If the plane is still in the hanger 90 percent of the time, I could lease her to a flight school to generate income from every hour they use the airplane. If the flight school uses the airplane just 10 hours per week (500 hours per year) and leases the airplane for $150 per hour, the airplane is generating $1,500 income every week or around $6,000 per month. With the total expenses of operating the airplane at $2,500 per month, now the plane is paying for itself and generating additional revenue for Kim and I. Even with the flight school using the airplane for 10 hours per week, she still sits in the hangar 80 percent of the time; Kim and I fly for free and the plane has become revenue-generating.

Why can't churches use their facilities the same way? Picture your ministry operating in a state-of-the-art facility, having 7/24 access to the spaces you need, while having other, like-minded groups use and pay for the facility. In addition, the other groups would bring people onto your campus where your ministry would have the opportunity to meet them, care for their needs, and provide them with the opportunity to engage with Christ.

Can Daycare Work For You?

Sounds a bit too good to be true, but it is happening. Last year, I was approached by a small, downtown church in Denver, Colorado, and asked to help with the development of their new facility. The church had purchased 3.5 acres in the Stapleton redevelopment area. The church bought the site for $800,000 and owed $750,000 on the land. They wanted me to design and build a new 30,000 square foot ministry center. The total project cost would be $4,250,000. When I visited the church, I was surprised to find only fifty people in the auditorium for the one and only Sunday morning service. The fifty included the pastors, choir, ushers, greeters, band members, and guest (me). How on earth can a church this small take on a $4.25 million project.? The answer was very simple: they cannot! If this project is ever going to happen, we needed to find someone else to pay the mortgage and operating expenses.

In studying the Stapleton area, I found the greatest need of young families moving into the community was for quality childcare and preschool. My experience has taught me over and over again that church run daycares and preschools are far from the best. The top of the line daycare and preschools are run by organizations like Tudor Time, Creme De La Creme, Primrose, Goddard Schools, and others. For this church to start up and operate a daycare might look good on paper, but in reality it would never measure up to the high standards of the Stapleton residences. So if the church lacks the experience and knowledge to run a top-notch daycare and preschool, then they should hire someone who does!

By hiring a professional daycare operator, we were able to do a preliminary feasibility study and determine the demand and price point for a daycare and preschool in the area. The feasibility study showed a substantial need for additional services and a fairly high price point. With this information, I designed a 30,000 square foot facility that will accommodate up to 200 children in daycare, preschool, along with before and after school programs for elementary-aged children. Our expert daycare and preschool consultant advised the leadership at the church that at 75 percent capacity, the operation could pay $35,000 per month for facility lease. In addition, the preschool and daycare would cover 100 percent of the utility bills and carry their own insurance.

Here is how the loan proceeds were to be dispersed at the church:

Pay off the balance owed on the property	$750,000
School furnishings and start up	$250,000
Site Work Development	$300,000
Soft Costs	$400,000
Building Costs	$2,300,000
Contingency for FF&E	$300,000
Total project cost	$4,300,000

At today's interest rates of 4 percent, the income from the daycare, preschool, and after-school activities would more than cover the building cost. The only real challenge was to design a building that can be built in today's dollars at $76 per square foot. To accomplish this, I went back to my early carpentry days with Goodman Church Builders and designed the most economical facility imaginable. It is a simple, wood-framed structure with long span wood trusses. It is a big house, using all residential construction methods. I don't foresee winning any AIA awards with this one, but the design still had to meet the rigorous standards of the Stapleton Homeowners Associations.

The end result is the church will be able to move into a brand new facility with a six hundred seat, multipurpose center, thirty thousand square feet of ministry space and never need to pay a mortgage, utility bill, or insurance premium!

Now, how do you take a really good deal and turn it into a fantastic deal? Let's look at other IPO your church could utilize.

The Kidzone Party Center

Most church facilities today, especially those with preschools and daycares, incorporate an indoor children's play area. I first designed one of these "Kidzones" into a church facility back in 1986 after taking my son, Brian, to the Discovery Zone in Los Gatos for his birthday. It did not take long for Brian to completely wear himself out as he climbed through balls and nets. At the time, I was volunteering on Sundays with the children's ministry at South Hills, and I couldn't help but wonder how a play structure like this would benefit the children's staff and volunteers by making good use of the abundant energy children possessed. After installing my first, multilevel, indoor play structure, I noticed it was a literal beehive of activity on Sunday, yet it sat mostly empty during the week.

After that, I recommended to the church that they remodel (a brand new environment) and make it available for birthday parties during the week. Following the remodel, the "Kidzone" became the most used room on the church campus. Members of the church were encouraged to have their children's birthday parties in the Kidzone area, which was remodeled to include tables, chairs, a small kitchenette, freezers for ice cream, and warming area for pizza. Parents invited kids from their neighborhoods, classmates from school to attend the birthday parties, and encouraged their parents to come as well. This brought large volumne of people to the church during the week who might not otherwise visit the church. Many churches have told me the parties and other Kidzone uses bring more unchurched people to their facility than almost any other program.

From an income perspective, the Kidzone and party room are free to "tithe paying" members. All others may utilize the party room in return for a reasonable donation. Now you have a great play structure for Sunday morning that generates revenue during the week.

Too Much Storage

In 1989, our hometown of Los Gatos was hit with a major earthquake. It happened during the World Series game between two of the Bay Area teams, the Oakland As and the San Francisco Giants. The earthquake measured 7.2 on the Richter Scale and was centered just three miles from our home. Kim was at home with our two boys (our daughter Jacqui was at Grandma's house) while I was attending a building committee meeting at South Hills in San Jose. Although many homes located in the hills above Los Gatos were totally destroyed, our home had no strcutural damage at all. (Goodman Church Builders had taught me how to build commercial buildings, and I never knew residential structures could be built using simpler and less expensive construction techniques. As a result, when Kim and I built our home in Los Gatos, I built it to commercial, earthquake-tolerant standards!)

The buildings in downtown Los Gatos did not hold up as well. Most of them were built in the 1890s and had undergone few, if any, seismic retrofits. One of my friends owned a building on Main Street. Their building collapsed entirely and was nothing more than a pile of rubble after the earthquake. I offered to redesign the building and build it back to the original 1893 look. This was a fun project, and I enjoyed being able to help my friends in getting their home and business back up and running. One of the challenges in rebuilding the facility was that the original structure had a basement with no permitted use. While the town allowed me to design and build the building back to the "pre-earthquake" condition, the town was very clear about the use of the basement. The Use Permit clearly stated we could not use the basement for retail space, office space, residential, industrial, or practically any use at all. The restrictions seemed so exhaustive it made no sense to build the basement. In fact, the only reason we did was because it was cheaper to include the basement than it was to bring in dirt-fill and build the building without it.

Once the new building was up and we had the retail and office spaces filled, we used the basement for the only thing the city had not disallowed: storage. Then it dawned on me. There was no commercial storage in downtown Los Gatos. I subdivided the basement using chain link fence (to not interfere with the fire sprinkler system) and leased out the entire basement as commercial mini-storage. This space cost very little to finish and ended up being the most profitable square footage of the entire facility.

Years later I was designing a church that was being built into a hill. The church did not need and could not afford to have a basement under it, but including an unfinished basement turned out to be the most economical way to build it. As a result of my experience in Los Gatos, I subdivided the church's basement into mini-storage and made it available for the congregation members to use. People took advantage of the space. They cleaned out their garages and even moved stuff from other mini-storage facilities to the space in the basement. People were encouraged to make a monthly donation to the church that would equal what they might pay elsewhere for storage. These donations just about covered the mortgage payment on the new facility!

As the church continued to grow, their dependency on the revenue generated from the storage became less, and the need for more ministry space increased. Over a period of time, the church was able to reclaim much of the storage area and transform the space into a new youth center. This worked out great, and I have been using this strategy for "storage" in facilities ever since.

God expects us to make the most of the assets and resources He provides for our ministries. No business in America would spend millions of dollars developing or buying a capital asset, only to let that asset sit empty or unused 95 percent of the time. We have to use ministry resources more effectively.

Do This: Partner with other like-minded ministries who will use your facility and offset the mortgage payment, utility payment, and insurance. Preschool, daycare, before-school and after-school programs, tutoring companies, gymnastic and martial arts classes all need space to conduct their activities. By making your unused space available, you generate additional funding for your ministry and invite the unchurched in your community onto your campus.

Don't Do This: While I encourage you to seek out income-producing opportunities, always be sure to do so in a way that does not jeopardize your tax-exempt status. Always consult a 501 C3 specialist when looking to partner with outside organizations in the use of your facility.

From First Time Guest to Raving Fan

Pastor Scott Burn raised a common question about how Kalamazoo Community Church could record 600-800 first time guest in one year and still have less than 500 people on a typical Sunday morning. It seemed their back door was seeing as many people out as the front door let in. So how could they close the back door?

At OASTER, we work with all types of Christian Churches from coast to coast. The congregations range in style from somewhat traditional to young, emerging, radical churches. They range in size from a few hundred to several thousand. The wide variety of churches we work with exposes us to the many different challenges faced by growing churches, and we get to participate in the creating unique solutions to overcome those difficulties.

As churches grow in size, a common occurrence begins to take place with first- and second-time guests. Often guests will not return. When asked about their decision to look elsewhere for a church (or not to go back to church at all), we often find these reasons:

- The church was too big, too impersonal
- I got lost in the crowd

- I felt like I did not belong
- The people were not friendly

Making a guest feel warm, invited, and welcomed takes a focused effort. Far too often a simple greeting from the pulpit is all they get. To enhance your guest's first-time visit to your church, you might consider developing a plan to make their first visit unforgettable. Here are some ideas we have picked up over the years to transform a first-time guest into a raving fan!

Signs and Directories

It is easy to take for granted the simple things everyone attending your church already knows. For example, where is your church? It might not be easy to locate if you have never been there before. Simple A-frame signs placed at major intersections can make your first-time guest much more comfortable getting to your church.

What does your entrance sign communicate? As you look through the various "church magazines," you see advertisements for sign companies marketing their products to churches. The signs usually look like a flashback to the fifties. It is hard to believe these companies actually sell these things to churches today! Next time you are out driving around your community, check out the new subdivisions, office parks, and shopping centers, and note how they present themselves through signage. Take a camera and photograph the church signs in your community. Put the photos on a board and study them. Now design a sign that totally reflects your ministry style. Don't let your church sign present the wrong image to the people you are trying to reach. Do something fresh and creative to expresses your style and core values.

Make your campus easy to navigate with on-site signs. A well-placed sign can show where your various buildings are located and direct guests to the proper parking areas. Clearly marked guest parking spaces will make visitors feel welcome and put them at ease. Install a large campus directory near the guest parking area. This will assist your guests in identifying the entrances and pertinent areas they are looking for. Each building should be clearly labeled on the outside wall. Labels such as Multipurpose Building, Main Auditorium, Chapel, Kid Kountry, etc., will help guests easily locate their destinations. Copies of the campus directory should also be placed in a weatherproof container attached to the main directory. Inside the church, a building directory with a map showing the building's floor plan will help visitors navigate through your facility.

First Impressions

When designing new facilities, keep the perspective of the first-time guest in mind. Make sure the building's appearance is warm and inviting. The main entry should be clearly visible from the parking lot and easily accessible to the elderly and handicapped. And position the restrooms in a visible, easy-to-find location. Be sure your nursery and café are in plain sight near the entry to your auditorium.

Parking Lot Attendants

Parking lot attendants can make finding a parking space and navigating the parking lot much easier. They should be happy people! Nothing makes visitors want to run away like a cranky parking lot attendant. Bright orange vests identify the attendants and flashlights make them visible at night. Your parking lot attendants will be the first people with whom guests come into contact at your church. You want to make sure that your guests and members enjoy a wonderful experience from start to finish.

"Finish" does not mean the end of the church service, rather when visitors and members have successfully navigated their way out of your parking lot and off campus.

Exit Signs

Have you been to a new McDonalds lately? When you exit the parking lot, you will see in bright white letters the words *thank you* painted on the asphalt. You might consider a similar sign posted at the exit of your parking lot. Some signs read, "You are now entering your mission field" or "God bless you and have a wonderful week." This is your last opportunity to send a positive message home with your guests and members.

Greeters

Greeters at the main entry can welcome your guests and assist them in locating specific destinations in your facility. A warm smile and a sincere hello can mean a lot to a person who is in an unfamiliar place. Your greeters should be comfortable and well-trained in finding out who visitors are, as well as in the layout of your facility. It would be pretty embarrassing if the greeters got lost!

Visitor Packets

Special packets can be prepared for both first- and second-time guests. When I worked with Santa Cruz Bible Church, they offered their guests a "Visitor's Survival Kit." Inside the kit was a letter of greeting from the pastor, Chip Ingram, along with a schedule of activities, campus map and floor plan of the facilities, descriptions of ministries and programs, and general information on the ministry at the church. You should also include a coupon for your café and have greeters looking for families who use the coupon.

Provide a Comfortable Atmosphere

One of the design flaws in many churches today is having a small foyer or one in the wrong location. The last thing you want your guests to do after the service is to walk through the foyer, grab the kids, and leave. Cutting-edge ministries make a concentrated effort to create a friendly diversion to guests who are on their way to the car. If guests leaving your auditorium walk through a large area with lots of natural light, with places to sit and talk while enjoying food and beverages, the odds of your guest hanging around for a while will greatly increase. Research shows if you can get a cup of coffee into the hands of your guest, they will stay around much longer. The longer they stay, the more comfortable they become, and the more likely they will come back. By the way, some churches purposely end their children's programs fifteen minutes after the main service lets out. This allows parents time to connect with new friends without feeling like they have to rush off to pick up the kids.

The Follow-Up Contacts

Contact from the church should reflect the kind of relationship you hope to nurture. In other words, if it is your desire to draw people into the family of God and to encourage the growth of their relationship to the Lord, your contact with them should communicate it in a personal way.

Follow-up contacts are great, but they should be done in a way that is both understood and appreciated. A nice card from you (the pastor) acknowledging their visit along with an invitation to "come back and see us again" is all it takes. Some churches have additional follow-up materials like a video outlining the purpose of the church, describing various programs, and with a message from you, the pastor. Some churches include a card listing coming upcoming sermon series.

Do This: Make everyone who enters the church doors feel welcomed and invited. Be sure to post helpful signs for guests. Help your guest feel informed. Have greeters at the door, visitor packets full of information. Follow-up with any new contacts.

Don't Do That: Leave the visitors to their own devices. Let the visitors wander around. If visitors want to come back, let them come back on their own.

Glossary of Terms

Pastors, church leaders, and building committee members who embark on a relocation of expansion project will be working with architects, builders, project managers, and other industry professionals who seem to speak their own language. As part of the goal of equipping you to not only understand this process but to lead the process, I have included this glossary of terms for your reference. Here are selected terms and definitions related to project delivery systems that you will most likely encounter when dealing with construction industry professionals. These definitions may vary from definitions used elsewhere, but this will give you the most common meaning of the terms. This Glossary is a compilation of many descriptions from various Public Works and City Planning Departments.

Addendum: A supplement to contract documents including additions or changes, usually issued following distribution of documents, but prior to acceptance of proposals by contractors.

Administrative relationship: A working condition between two parties that is not contractual but which entails transfer of valuable services and information.

Advanced purchasing: A legal notice in a journal of general circulation soliciting proposals for a construction project; required for public sector projects and aimed as objectivity and marketplace economics in selecting contractors.

Affidavit: A written sworn statement, submitted by a contractor with application for payment as part of the documentation of work completed and disbursement of funds, intended to assure payers (owners and lenders) that suppliers, subcontractors, and worker have been duly paid and will not seek further payment, possibly through liens, from the payer.

Agent: One who is empowered to act in behalf of and in the best interests of another for prescribed activity. Agency is the act or quality of being an agent.

Agreement, form of agreement: A document setting forth the provisions, responsibilities, and obligations of parties to a contract. Standard forms of agreement for building construction are available from the American Institute of Architects and the Associated General Contractors of America and are designed to allow the insertion of data relevant to particular projects.

Alliance: A long-term relationship between parties for services on several projects. Owner-contractor alliances are sometimes called partnering or preferred suppliers.

Allowance: A sum of money stated in the contract documents to cover the cost of materials or items in those documents, the full description of which is not known at the time of bidding. All contractors bid the allowance as part of their proposals. The actual costs of the items are determined by the contractor (not including installation) at the time of their selection by architect or owner, and the total contractual amount is adjusted accordingly. Examples: brick, carpet, appliances.

Alteration Work: Changes and additions to existing facilities; remodeling; retrofitting.

Alternative Dispute Resolution (ADR): A range of procedures that are options to work stoppages, alienation of parties, and litigation, with the objective of resolving problems before they negatively affect contractual relationships, schedule, and productivity. Ideally, an ADR provision should be included either in the contract or in a partnering charter. Examples, in general order of increasing seriousness, include:

> **Negotiation:** A semi-formal process in which parties directly involved in a disagreement meet, ideally away from the distraction of the job site, to attempt to resolve differences with a minimum of aggravation and energy, and to avoid full-blown dispute.

> **Mediation:** Negotiation aided by a neutral third party whose role is to establish key facts in the dispute and to guide the disputants to resolution. The mediator has no binding powers.

> **Medarb:** A hybrid of mediation and arbitration wherein the disputants agree ahead of time to allow the mediation process to move directly into arbitration of mediation is unsuccessful.

> **Dispute Board:** A panel of people (usually three) who are knowledgeable of both construction and the law, appointed prior to a project, and then called upon to hear and decide disputes when they occur. Whether or not their decisions are binding depends on the language in the agreement that sets up the dispute board.

> **Mini-Trial:** Simulated trial in which key information is places before executives of disputing parties, allowing

them to predict the outcome of real litigation and thus possibly agree to a negotiated settlement.

Arbitration: A formal process that engages a single arbitrator or a three-person panel with binding powers to decide a dispute. The process typically includes legal representation of the parties, introduction of evidence, testimony by witnesses, etc. If standard procedures are following (such as those promulgated by the American Arbitration Association), courts typically honor arbitrated decisions.

American Institute of Architects: A national association that promotes principles, standards, and activities that are important to the practice of architecture, including ethics, education, legislation, and professional advice. The AIA also publishes many documents that guide design and construction processes.

American Subcontractors Association: A national trade association made up of member companies which perform traditional trade work.

Application for Payment: A formal submittal by a contractor or subcontractor for payment for work performed within a particular period, usually each month, which may include materials purchased and property stored. The form of application, timing, and documentation are stated in the agreement.

Architect: A professional person who is duly licensed by a state (by examination or reciprocity) to perform services in that state involving the design of buildings.

Architect-Engineer: A term frequently used to designate a design professional when it is not clear which shall be retained, an architect or engineer. AE is the frequent abbreviation to describe a designed or design firm. Very few persons are both architects and engineers.

As-Built Drawings: See "record drawings."

Assignment: The transfer of rights or responsibilities, or the placement of contractual obligations by one person or another. Frequently, prime trade contractors are assigned by an owner to general contractor or construction manager to better coordinate the execution of a construction project.

Association: An organization established to serve the interests of similar parties. Examples are trade associations, manufacturers' associations, and vendors' associations.

Associated General Contractors of America: A national trade association made up primarily of general contracting companies but also including related occupations and professions. There are four divisions: Building, Highway, Heavy & Industrial, and Municipal-Utilities.

Associated Specialty Contractors of America: A national trade association made up of companies supplying and performing specialized materials and services.

Award: The act by one party of granting a contractual opportunity to another party typically as a response to a proposal, as in an owner awarding a contract to a low bidder or a general contractor awarding a subcontract.

Back Charge: A claim of one contractor against another contractor or subcontractor for work done or not done or for interference or delay, thus causing the charging contractor with loss or delay.

Bar Chart: See, "schedule."

Bar Coding: A method of identifying materials or components with a laser readable code attached to the objects. It is helpful in establishing inventories and locations of materials.

Basic Service: Those provided under typical agreements, as differentiated from extra or comprehensive services.

Bid: A proposal submitted in various forms, oral or written, to perform remunerative work or to buy an object. Related definitions in construction are:

> **Bid, Competitive:** Proposals are compared to each other on some prescribed basis, such as a set of contract documents, and the "lowest and best" bid is usually accepted.

> **Bid Day or Bid Date:** The date set by the owner or architect, usually with definite _____ when competitive bids are due.

> **Bid Depository:** Secure place where trade and material bids may be received and picked up by general contractors; usually maintained by an agency.

> **Bid Form, Form of Proposal:** Official document used for submittal of competitive bids.

> **Bid Guarantee, Bid Security:** A bid bond or certified check, cashier's check, or similar instrument to assure an owner that a bid is valid and that the bidder will enter into a contract if awarded. Refusal to enter into a contract leads to a forfeiture of the guarantee.

Bid Period: The time between announcement or advertisement of a project available for bidding and the bid date. The bid period is statutory in public work.

Bid Requirements: Instructions to bidders; the written prescription of how bidders shall submit proposals and what to include.

Bid, Responsive or Non-Responsive: Characterization of a bid as either meeting all the bid requirements or not meeting such. Non-responsive bids may not be accepted by public owners.

Bid Shopping, Bid Peddling: The practice by a few general contractors of continuing to shop for lower bids from subcontractors after receiving initial bids from those and other subcontractors, sometimes exposing (peddling) the bids of competitors in the process. Subcontractors also sometimes "shop around" to determine competitors' bids and then offer second or third proposals. These practices are considered unethical but not illegal.

Bills of Materials: Schedules or lists prepared by contractors or subcontractors of materials needed for all or part of a project.

Blueprint: A reproduction of a drawing based on the process of producing a negative image on light sensitive paper. It has become the vernacular term for an architectural drawing or any plan of execution whether drawn, written or otherwise described.

Boilerplate: A vernacular term for the language in contracts or insurance policies that describes in detail the obligations of the parties; also sometimes called the "fine print."

Bond: A written agreement containing a financial guarantee that one party, the surety, obligates itself to a second party, the oblige (usually an owner), to assure the performance, service, or payment by another party, the principal (usually a contractor and sometimes called an obligor). Various types of bonds and related items are offered below as supplied by the Surety Association of America.

> **Aggregate Liability Clause:** A clause in a surety bond that limits the surety's liability to the amount of the bond penalty regardless of the number of claims made against the bond.

> **Bid Bond:** A bond given by a bidder to accompany a construction or supply contract to guarantee that the bidder, if awarded the contract within the time stipulated, will enter into the contract and furnish any prescribed performance and payment bond. Default (not proceeding after being awarded a contract) will ordinarily result in liability to oblige for the difference between the amount of the principal's bid and the bid of the next lowest bidder who can qualify for the contract. In any event, however, the liability of the surety is limited to the bid bond penalty.

> **Bonding Capacity:** The limit of bonded work that a contractor can perform; a function of the willingness of a surety to provide bonding.

> **Cancellation Clause:** A clause in a bond that terminates the surety's future liability.

> **Collateral:** Anything of a value pledged to the surety to protect the surety against loss by a reason of default by the principal.

Completion Bond: A bond covering performance of a construction project that names as an obligee a lender or other party in a position to invoke the performance features of the bond without an obligation to provide funds to complete the project.

Continuous Bond: A bond that remains in force and effect until cancelled.

Contract Bond: A bond given to secure the performance of a contract. Frequently, two parts are required; one part of the bond coves performance and the other part covers payment of certain labor and material bills. (Note: this is essentially a combination of performance, labor, and material payment bonds, both of which are discussed in following definitions.)

Contract Price: The entire sum of money that passes from the owner to the contractor when final settlement is made between the parties to the contract. It is used as the basis for the bond premium charge on most types of construction and supply contract bonds.

Corporate Surety: A corporation licensed under various insurance laws, which within its charger has legal power to act as surety for others.

Cost Bond: A bond required of a litigant conditioned for the payment of the cost of the litigation, such as fees of the court clerk, sheriff, and the like.

Co-Surety: An arrangement where two or more surety companies directly participate on a bond.

Cumulative Liability: The aggregate amount recoverable under two or more bonds in behalf of the same principal filed in succession, where the succeeding bond(s) does not extinguish the liability under the prior bond(s).

Customs Bond: guarantees the payment of import duties and taxes and compliance with regulations governing the entry into the United States of merchandise from foreign countries.

Effective Date: The date from which coverage is provided.

Expiration Date: The date upon which a bond or policy will cease to provide coverage.

Fiduciary Bond: Covers public officials, company officers, or license holders who have obligations to the general public stockholders.

Indemnity: An agreement whereby the principal or others agree to make reimbursement to the surety for any loss the surety may incur under the bond.

Indemnitor: One who enters into an agreement with a surety company to hold the surety harmless from any loss or expense it may sustain or incur on a bond issued to another on behalf of the indemnitor.

Labor and Material (Payment) Bond: A bond given by a contractor to guarantee payment to certain laborers, subcontractors, and suppliers for the labor and material used in the work performed under the contract. This liability may be continued in the performance bond, in which case a separate labor and material bond (payment bond) is not given.

Liability: A bond term denoting any legally enforceable obligation.

License Bond: Used interchangeably with the term "permit bond" to describe bonds required by state law, municipal ordinances, or regulations to be filed prior to the particular privilege. Such bonds provide payment to the oblige or, in some instances, to third parties for loss, damage resulting from violations by the licensee of the duties, and obligations imposed by the license or permit.

Maintenance Bond: The normal coverage provided by a maintenance bond guarantees against defective workmanship or materials. However, maintenance bonds may occasionally incorporate any obligation guaranteeing "efficient or successful operation" or other obligations of the like intent and purpose.

Mechanics Lien-Bond to Discharge: A lien against real estate may be filed for an amount claimed to be due for labor or materials furnished for the construction of a building or other improvement upon the property. Pending the final determination of the owner's liability, the owner may discharge the lien by giving a bond conditioned for the payment of any amount that may be legally found due to the claimant, with interest and cost.

Miller Act Bond: A performance bond and labor material payment bond required by the Miller Act on public work of the United States, as approved August 24, 1935. (Reference:40 U. S.C./270a)

Obligee: The party to whom a bond is given; the party protected against loss. An oblige may be a person, firm, corporation, government, or agency.

Performance Bond: A bond that guarantees performance of the terms of a written contract. Performance bonds sometimes incorporate payment bonds (labor and materials) and maintenance bond liabilities.

Personal Surety: An individual who acts as surety for another, who may or may not charge a fee for his or her guarantee. Unlike corporate sureties, which are closely regulated and licensed, person sureties are generally not submit to any government regulation or licensing requirements.

Premium: The feel to be paid for the bond.

Premium Earned: The premium amount that would compensate the surety for the protection furnished for the expired portion of the bond item.

Premium Unearned: Tat part of the premium that has not yet been earned by the surety for the unexpired portion of the term of the bond.

Principal: The one who is primarily bound on a bond furnished by a surety company. For example, in a contract bond, the principal is the contractor; in a public official bond, the principal is the public official; in a fiduciary bond, the principal is the one who carries the obligation or license. Sometimes the principal is called the obligor.

Rider: A printed manuscript form attached to a bond to add to, alter, or vary the bond's provisions.

Salvage: That which is recovered from the principal or an indemnitor to offset in whole, or in part, the loss and expense incurred by a surety in satisfying obligations it has sustained under a bond.

Statutory Bond: Generally described as a bond given in compliance with a statute. Such a bond must carry whatever liability the statute imposes on the principal and the surety.

Subcontract Bond: A bond required of a subcontractor by a general contractor, guaranteeing that the subcontractor will fully perform the subcontract in accordance with its terms and will pay for certain labor and materials incurred in the execution of the subcontracted work.

Subdivision Bond: A bond guaranteeing a construct or finance an improvement such as a street, sidewalk, curb, gutter, or sewer or drainage.

Supply Bond: A bond that guarantees performance of a contract to furnish supplies or materials. In the event of a default by the supplier, the surety must indemnify the purchases of the supplied party against any loss occasioned thereby.

Surety Bond: A written agreement providing for monetary replacement compensation to be paid by the surety should there be a failure by the person bonded to perform specified acts within a stated period.

Suretyship: Refers to obligations to pay the debt of, or answer for the default or miscarriage of another. It is a legal relationship based upon a written contract in which one person or corporation (the surety) undertakes to answer to another (the oblige) for the debt, default, or miscarriage of a third person (the principal) resulting from the third person's failure to pay or perform as required by an underlying contract, permit, ordinance, law, rule, or regulation.

Third Party Bond: A license bond that gives parties to other than the named oblige a right of action in their own name to recover loss or damage resulting from a breach by the licensee of its obligations under the law, ordinance, or regulation under which the bond is required.

Underwriter: An officer or employee of a surety company who has the responsibility for accepting or rejecting risk.

Bonds, As Financial Instruments: An obligation of one party to pay a prescribed amount, usually plus interest, to another party in return for capital use for construction or major purchases. Thus, hospital bonds may be purchased by investors to provide construction capital, with the binding agreement that interest will be paid on the bonded amount until the face values of the bonds are returned to the investor at the conclusion of the agreed upon terms.

Bridging: A hybrid project delivery system wherein a designer completes schematics and partial design development, and then the owner requests proposals for completion of documents and construction from design-build contractors.

Brochure: Illustrated document, part marketing, part informational, used to describe products, capabilities, or companies.

Building Authority: The governmental agency or person who enforces building codes through plan reviews, field inspections, and code interpretations.

Building Board of Standards; Board of Appeals: An agency that promulgates and updates codes and renders decisions to appeals by designers, owners, or contractors (different titles in different jurisdictions).

Building Codes: Legislated statutes by state and local governments, under their police power, to regulate design and construction to protect the health and safety of citizens. Codes are most concerned with fire protection, safe engress from buildings, structural stability, and sanitation. Special subsets of codes cover plumbing, HVAC, fire protection, and elevators.

Building Commissioner: Chief officer of building authority, usually having broad authority over code interpretations, document approval, granding of permits, and field inspections. Alternative titles are Chief Building Inspector, Building Official, etc.

Building Permit: A regulatory device employed by building authorities to enforce building, zoning, environmental, and other legislated codes. Drawings and specifications must be submitted for review and must meet all applicable codes for permit to be issued. Similar permits are issued for specialty work such as plumbing, HVAC, electrical, elevators, etc., usually by subagencies of the building authority. Temporary or conditional permits may be issued for accelerated work or for other cases where a start of construction prior to completed documents is desired by the contractor and allowed by the building authority. Fees are charged for all permits and are theoretically in an amount to cover the activity of the building authority, including field inspection.

CAD(D): Computer aided drafting (and design); a general term for a wide array of operations and techniques.

Capital: Funds used for any purpose, including construction. Capital costs in a project cover land, construction, and fees, as compared to maintenance costs or life cycle costs. Capitalization refers to the financial ability of a party to fund an activity, such as a contractor capitalizing on a project prior to the first payment by the owner.

Cardinal Change: A major amendment to a contract, typically expanding the project scope.

Cash Allowance: See "allowance."

Cash Discount: Reduced cost for prompt payment.

Cash Flow: Income stream for projects; a measure of liquidity.

Catalog: A compendium of information, usually illustrated, about a product or range of products used by designers and contractors to help select and properly install building components. Catalog "cuts" (illustrations) containing descriptive information about products are frequently part of submittals for approval during construction.

Certificate of Materialmen: A statement by a material supplier listing dollar amounts of supplies provided to a project in a particular period; may be required in applications for payment submitted to the owner by the contractor.

Certificate of Occupancy (CO): A regulatory device employed by building authorities to assure that all code requirements are met prior to occupying a building. Conditional COs may be granted for a phased move-in by the owner. CO fees are usually part of the building permit fees. The architect or contractor typically notifies the building authority to request a final inspection for a CO.

Certification: A process of designating persons as being competent in occupations or activities. A certified welder, for instance, has received a certain amount of training and has passed one or more tests to demonstrate competency and then becomes a "certified welder."

Certification (Second Definition): Approval by one party of the action or application of another party, as in architect certifying an application for payment by a contractor.

Change Order: Amendment to a contract based on a change initiated by the owner, designer, contractor, or building official and documented by a written amendment signed by the owner and contractor after price and schedule adjustment are agreed upon.

Close-Out: A process of completing a construction project and turning it over to the owner. It is usually a multi-work sequence of approvals, partial occupancies, a punch list, documentation, and celebrations.

Code: A body of regulations initiated by legislatures and promulgated by various officials, usually under the police power of government to regulate health and safety. Codes that regulate construction include building codes, fire codes, environmental codes, electrical codes, and zoning codes.

Commission: An agreement whereby one party requests and rewards services from another party, as in an owner awarding a design commission to an architect.

Commissioning: A process of assuring that all equipment is working properly and that operators are trained in use of equipment. This may be part of the services of designers or constructors under a special contractual agreement with the owners.

Completion: Finalization of a project and conclusion of a contract. Substantial completion is the condition when gainful occupancy may be taken by the owner or users and when final payment (except retainage) is ordinarily made to the contractor. Final completion is when a project is thoroughly completed, including all punch list items, and is "closed out." The contractor receives all remaining payment due upon final completion. Both completions are usually certified by the architect.

Comprehensive Services: A term relating to a full range of services provided by a designer or contractor beyond the "basic services" ordinarily described in an agreement with an owner. An architect's comprehensive services may include land planning, programming, feasibility studies, financing, and special consulting. A contractor's comprehensive services may include those same items plus site selection, land acquisition, commissioning, start-up, and maintenance.

Conditions: A broad term used to describe a number of situations and relationships in construction:

> **General Conditions:** The part of contract documents that describe in detail the relationships and obligations of the parties. A frequently used standard form is AIA

A201, *General Conditions of the Contract for Construction.* Related general conditions refer to the support and coordination elements on a job site, including temporary facilities, security, signage, reporting, and parts of management and supervision.

Special Conditions: The part of the contract documents that describes aspects peculiar to a project.

Supplemental (Supplementary) Conditions: Usually elaborates on general conditions.

Conditions of Acceptance: Pertains to many circumstances wherein one party sets limits on acceptability of performance by another party.

Conditions of Proposal, Bid Conditions: Included in the instructions to the bidders or the advertisement for bids to explain the requirements for a responsive bid.

Condominium: A form of real estate ownership in which an occupant has full title to a unit (space) and membership in an association for ownership of common areas.

Constructability: A design review process by experienced constructors and designers with the objective of establishing during design rational and efficient construction procedures for field execution. The ultimate aim is to cause the designer to adopt materials, systems, and details that are both cost effective and time effective in the field without sacrificing aesthetic intent. Constructability is frequently combined with value engineering as a review process.

Construction: A general term for a multitude of activities that integrate to become a built product. The term is normally applied to the industry responsible for constructing the vast array of buildings, public works, and monuments of modern society. Branches of construction include:

> **Building Construction:** The segment of the construction involved in commercial, institutional, and some industrial buildings, but excluding houses.

> **Heavy and Highway Construction:** Related to roads, bridges, dams, airports, etc.; sometimes called civil construction.

> **Industrial Construction:** Factories, refineries, power plants, etc.

> **Public Works Construction:** Related to service facilities such as water treatment and sewage disposal plants.

> **Residential Construction:** Primarily home building but may also include multi-family and group housing.

Construction Management: A project delivery system based on an agreement whereby the construction entity provides leadership to the construction process through a series of services to the owner, including design review, overall scheduling, cost control, value engineering, constructability, preparation of bid packages, and construction coordination. In *agency CM*, the construction entity is typically retained at the same time as the design team and provides continuous services to the owner without taking on financial risks for the execution of the actual construction. In *at-risk CM*, the construction entity, after providing agency services during the pre-construction period, takes on the financial obligation to carry out construction under a specified cost agreement. A guaranteed maximum price is frequently provided by the construction in at-risk CM. At-risk CM is sometime called CM/GC because the construction entity becomes essentially a general contractor through the at-risk agreement.

Constructor: The term adopted by practitioners who execute construction to define the persons who are responsible for all or part of the building process. In some contracts constructors used to designate the party directly responsible for the execution of a project.

Contingency: Something uncertain but probably; in planning or budgeting contingency items or costs are included for anticipated events, the details of which are unknown in advance.

Contingency Fund: An amount of money set aside in anticipation of costs beyond a target price or contractual amount. Contingency funds are important in any agreement with a guaranteed maximum price. Following are types of contingencies used with GMPs (one, two, or three may be used):

> **Design Contingency:** A fund of money established to absorb cost growth during the design process.
>
> **Owner's Contingency:** A fund to cover cost growth during design or construction and used only with the approval of the owner; usually used for items requested by the owner.
>
> **Contractor's or Construction Manager's Contingency:** A fund to cover cost growth during design or construction and used in the discretion of the contractor or construction

manager, usually for costs that are the result of a project circumstances rather than any one party's instigation.

Contract: A binding agreement between two parties describing obligations of both parties. Contracts may be based on a variety of forms and conditions, from handshakes to complex documents. Most construction contracts are based on standard forms of agreement provided by associations such as the American Institute of Architects and the Associated General Contractors of America. Some owners generate their own contract forms. Standard forms have the advantage of being broadly recognized instruments with clauses that have evolved over time due to dispute resolution and court tests.

Contract Documents: The drawings, specifications, and attendant documents that make up the total agreement and obligations between owner and contractor. Sometimes called construction documents, they describe in advance the finished product to result from the contract.

Contractor: A person or company who accepts responsibility to perform the obligations of a contract; a term usually applied to one who engages in contract execution as a regular employment. More specific terms include:

> **Construction Contractor:** A person or company who performs construction as a business.

> **General Contractor:** An entity that takes responsibility for whole projects through agreements with owners.

Prime Contractor: One who has a contract directly with an owner.

Subcontractor: One who has a contract with a prime contractor.

Specialty Contractor: An entity that focuses on trade work that entails particular skills, such as control systems, ornamental works, and finishes; sometimes the term is used interchangeably with trade contractor.

Trade Contractor: An entity that performs one or more traditional branches of work, such as masonry, roofing, or carpentry; usually works as a subcontractor to a general contractor but may take on prime contracts directly with an owner, as is frequently the case in agency construction management.

Coordination: Part of the administrative and management duties performed by a contractor or construction manager to schedule, advise, and guide other parties such as subcontractors and tradespersons; usually directly performed on side by a project superintendant.

Corporation: A business organization that creates a legal entity separate from individual participants and owned by stockholders or shareholders. Corporations have the effect of continuing an organization that participants change and of providing a mechanism to partially shield individuals from liability. Articles of incorporation must be filed with the appropriate p, and officers and shareholders must be identified. Most construction companies are closely held corporations, which means that the shares are retained by a small group of people, are not actively traded, and usually contain provisions for returning shares to the company upon resignation, retirement, or death of a shareholder.

Cost Control: The process that seeks to ensure that actual costs do not exceed estimated costs, or the efforts to seek the lowest possible costs during both the design and construction phases.

Cost, Cost Accounting: Accumulating the actual costs of labor and materials for purposes of billing the work, comparing job costs to the project estimate, and upgrading historical records; usually done under a numerical coding system.

Cost-Plus a Fee Contract: The project delivery system whereby a contractor and owner negotiate an agreement, the pertinent aspects of which are that the costs of labor and material are billed to the owner plus the contractors overhead and profit, the latter of which is a fixed fee or a percentage of the costs.

Critical Path: See "scheduling."

Daily Log: Part of a document system; a journal with entries inserted each work day listing activities accomplished, weather, visitors, problems encountered, and any other pertinent information that may be valuable for future reconstruction of events. The daily log is the responsibility of the site superintendent.

Data Bank: Sometimes used interchangeably with the term database, it is more descriptive of the computer programming capability of placing information in storage.

Dedication: The act or process of establishing a particular use of building, systems, or parts of infrastructure, such as the dedication of streets to public use, which means that a unit of government agrees to accept ownership of the street and will thus maintain it.

Default: A condition wherein a party to a contract fails to complete the terms of the contract. The most frequent construction situation is when a contractor fails to complete the contracted work and is declared by a third party, such as the architect, to be unable to continue adequate performance.

Design: A process of composing ideas and requirements into an understandable scheme or plan for a product. Building design involves architects, engineers, consultants, and sometimes constructors working together to develop drawings and written descriptions (specifications) for a building. Architectural design terms and phrases, generally in the order in which they occur, include:

> **Programming:** Typically done prior to the design process, but sometimes integrated with early design procedures, programming clarifies objectives of the proposed building and lays a strategy for the design and construction process.
>
> **Diagrammatics:** Single line drawings indicating spaces, shapes, circulation patterns, and perhaps massing. Sometimes called pre-schematics, they are usually accompanied by a schedule of spaces and budget.
>
> **Esquisse:** A Beaux Arts term still occasionally used to describe a creative sketch process.
>
> **Schematics:** Accurate, pictorial drawings indicating all of the elements shown in diagrammatics but with more information including materials, sizes, colors, and aesthetic factors; may include color renderings and models and usually accompanied by outline specifications and preliminary estimate. Owner approval is required to proceed with the next phase.
>
> **Design Development:** The information from the schematic stage is further investigated; materials and components are further researched and compared, and detail drawings are undertaken; specifications are begun,

and an updated estimate is given by the architect. Value engineering and constructability are frequently performed during design development by a team including designers, constructors, and consultants. (Owner approval may be required to proceed to the next stage.)

Contract Documents: A continuum with design development in which fully detailed drawings, specifications, and attendant documents are produced in preparation for accurate pricing by contractors and execution of construction.

Contract Administration: Extension of design duties into the construction stage, during which architects and engineers maintain liaison with contracts and monitor the jobsite to interpret the contract documents and to act as the owner's agent in reviewing construction proceedings.

Mechanical Design: Related to plumbing, fire suppression, and HVAC systems.

Environment Design: A general term for broad scope planning and design for the total human environment. Sometimes also used to describe HVAC design.

Electrical Design: Related to power, light , controls, and systems.
Interior Design: Limited to interiors, with emphasis on materials and finishes.

Space Design: More comprehensive than interior design; includes studies of interior functions, relationships, and activity in spaces.

Specialized Design: Includes acoustics, ergonomics, fire protection, and other specialties.

Design-Build: A project-delivery system based on an agreement whereby the design service and construction service are formed into a single entity and that entity is obligated to the owner for the combined services. The design services may be provided by in-house designers employed by the construction company or by retained consultative designers. Design-build-lease, turnkey, and bridging are types of design-build contracts.

Developer: An entrepreneur who invests in land and buildings and who sometimes manages the construction involved in those investments.

Directive: A written order issued by one party to another, such as an architect to a contractor, usually to document a vocal order. See "Field order."

Disadvantaged Business Enterprise (DBE): A term that subsumes minority business enterprise and women's business enterprise and usually relates to governmental regulations for contracting or employment.

Documentation: A general term describing the preservation and enumeration of information for a variety of uses, such as to back-up application for payment to provide a written record of a project, and to help settle disputes.

Draw: Applications for payment; a contractor periodically "draws" upon the amount of money in the contractual agreement.

Drawings: Graphic documents that describe a project, which types ranging from sketches to the fully detailed set of drawings that make up a principal component of contract documents.

Egress: A mean of exiting a building or a job site; linked to safety and compliance.

Experience Modifier Ratio (EMR): Tool for measuring contractors safety.

Engineer: A professional person who is duly licensed by a state (by examination or reciprocity) to perform services in that state involving the design of buildings, transportation systems, environmental facilities, etc. There are many specialties within engineering. Licenses are renewable, are policed to some degree by state boards, and are revocable upon breaches of professional conduct. (The term *engineer* is sometimes used generically for any person who designs, implements, or evaluates technical systems or equipment, but legally one must be licensed to use the term.)

Ergonomics: The relationships of persons to their immediate environments, and the study thereof related to biotechnology. In design and construction, it deals with composing workspaces to maximize positive control and interaction of workers to their spaces and equipment.

Estimating: Forecasting the costs of labor, materials, equipment, and related items prior to their actual execution, usually based on units of historical data in the contractor's files, published indexes, and information supplied by subcontractors and suppliers. A general contractor must determine which segments of a job should be a bid in-house and which segments should depend on prices from specialty contractors. A formal bid is the total project estimate plus mark-ups for overhead, profit, and contingencies. In vernacular terms, contractors say that the estimate is the cost of buying a job, and the bid is the price of selling the job to the owner.

Ethics: Beliefs, attitudes, and behaviors that are based on honesty, integrity, and fair dealing. Many businesses and professions have codes of ethics to guide behavior. The American Institute of Constructors and the Associated General Contractors of America all have codes of ethics. Courts have determined that codes may not impede free trade, such as competitive pricing.

Extra; Extra Work: A vernacular term for labor and materials beyond that described in a construction contract and which usually involves change orders.

Fast-Track: Accelerated scheduling that involves commencing construction prior to the completion of contract documents and then using means such a bid packages and efficient coordination to compress the overall schedule. See "Phased Construction."

Feasibility, Feasibility Study: Related to advisability of engaging an operation or project based on its probability of success, particularly from a financial aspect.

Fee: Payment for work or services, usually negotiated in advance between parties. Fees can be based on a number of arrangements, including a fixed amount, percentage of the cost of the work or services, hourly rate, value of services, or a combination of factors. Contractors sometimes call the profit margin placed on the bid the fee.

Field; Fieldwork, Field office: The terms for the location and efforts directly related to job sites, as differentiated from home office operations.

Field Order: Issued by the architect or engineer to the contractor as a directive to carry out some aspect of a project that may not be clear in the contract documents or that may be a change from those documents. If significance or involving increased costs or time, a field order should lead to a change order.

Final: Completion, conclusion of a project; vernacular term for final acceptance and payment.

Fire Protection: A broad array of consideration in building design, code compliance, job safety, emergency services, and fire suppression.

Force Account: A contractual term describing an agreement where the owner orders work to be done by direct employees or the contractor without prior agreement on final price, with payment to be based on the costs of labor, materials, overhead, and profit.

Force Majeure: An unforeseen event of major impact and the related consequences, particularly as those consequences might affect a project schedule or cost.

Front-End Loading; Front-Loading: A tactic by a contractor to place an artificially high value (in the schedule of values) on early activities to improve cash flow. This practice should be avoided by assigning a reasonable value to be placed on mobilization, on general conditions, and on early procurement of materials.

General Conditions: See "conditions."

General Requirements: A specifications section describing activities that are necessary to carry out a project but that are not directly related to trade work.

Guarantee: An assurance of quality of work or value of services for a set period of time, and legally enforceable. Most building contracts call for a one-year guarantee of completed buildings. Components and equipment may carry longer guarantees or warranties.

Guaranteed Maximum Price (GMP): An amount established in an agreement for a project where the exact costs are not known at the time of agreement, the final costs are anticipated to be equal to or lower than the GMP, and the contractor must absorb any costs above the GMP.

Hard Bid, Hard Money Bid: Vernacular term for lump-sum price.

Historical Data: Information that a company builds up over time to assist in planning and estimating future activity.

Hold Harmless Clause: A statement in a contract that describes the indemnification of any owner by a contractor wherein the contractor agrees to shield the owner from liability for actions of the contractor or other parties. Similar clauses in subcontracts protect contractors from actions of subcontractors.

Incentive Clause: A contractual inclusion that provides payments beyond the stated amount in the contract if completion is ahead of schedule or if other objectives are reached that may involve costs savings, safety, quality, or absence of disputes. Incentive clauses are much more frequent in private work than in public work.

Indemnification: Action or agreement whereby one party secures another party against loss, such as a contractor indemnifying an owner (possibly with a hold harmless clause) or a contractor indemnifying a surety as a condition of receiving a bond.

Inspection: Examination of buildings and other products to determine their compliance with specifications or contract requirements; related to approvals by building officials for code compliance and permission to occupy a completed building.

Instruction to Bidders: A segment of the contract documents with directions on how to compile and submit a responsive bid.

Insurance: Coverage through an agreement (contract) whereby one party insures (underwrites, provides coverage) to guarantee against losses of another party that may result from perils specified in the agreement. Insurance types and terms are as follows:

> **Builders Risk:** Purchased by the owner to cover property and casualty loss and liability related to the project.

> **Contractor's Auto Liability:** Coverage for owned or leased autos or those driven on behalf of the contractor, for bodily injury, property damage, uninsured motorist, collision, and comprehensive damage.

> **Professional Liability:** Coverage for services rendered by the designer and sometimes called errors and omissions insurance; an important coverage in design-build projects (not included in wrap-up packages).

Subcontractors' Insurance: Similar to that of contractors.

> **Workers' Compensation:** Coverage for injury, death, or illness of employees or benefits to their survivors; required in all states.

Wrap-Up: One policy to cover all exposures on an entire project (except workers' compensation in monopolistic states); usually purchased by the owner.

ISO: International Standards Organization; agency that coordinates measuring systems and quality efforts on an international basis, including the metric system.

Invitation to Bid: Invited Bid List: Pertaining to solicitation of competitive bids from a select group of contractors, usually in the private sector.

Job: Vernacular term for a construction project; frequently used in such other terms as job-site, job costs, and job-related activity.

Joint Venture: A contractual collaboration of two or more parties to undertake a project, examples being: an architect-architect, an architect-contractor, and a contractor-contractor.

Labor; Labor Costs: The human resource aspect of construction; the segment of work and costs represented by a human effort, as compared to materials or indirect costs.

Labor Union: An organization of tradespersons or laborers that represents the interests of members to employers, particularly in collective bargaining for unified working conditions and wages.

Letter of Credit: An instrument of borrowing frequently used by contractors to establish the availability of funds for their operations. It becomes a demand instrument by the bank and may be payable to the owner in case of default by the contractor.

Liability: A term describing a party's potential legal exposure for responsibilities, acts, omissions, happenings, etc., which may be damaging to other parties. Ordinarily all parties carry insurance to cover exposure to liability.

Licenses: The legal authority granted by states to practice a profession or occupation within that state. All states require licensed professionals, architect or engineers, to design building, with the exception in some states of residential buildings. Also, many governments require licenses of contractors and certain trades such as plumbers and electricians.

Lien: A legal encumbrance against real or financial property for work, material, or services rendered to provide value to that property. Related items:

> **Lien Foreclosure; Perfection of a Lien:** A legal process usually involving a suit in a court of law to fore an owner to pay the state amount of lien.
>
> **Lien Waiver:** Action by which a party waives rights to place a lien, usually specific to portion of payment received. Each time a supplier or contractor is paid, the owner may require a waiver of lien for that amount of payment and will further expect a complete waiver of lien upon final payment.
>
> **Mechanic's Lien; Mechanic's Lien Law:** The basis of most construction liens. State Laws provide procedures for workers, suppliers, and contractors to encumber property and foreclosure liens in order to get paid for their contributions for value of property. Laws stipulate the procedures, forms, and time periods for liens.
>
> **Release of Lien:** An action by one who had filed a lien, after having been satisfied payment or otherwise, to release the property owner of further obligation.

Tax Lien: Filed by governmental agencies on property or funds, of parties believed to owe taxes.

Life Cycle Costing: An evaluative process aimed at projecting the costs of building components and operation over time. Factors include capital (initial) costs, replacement costs, maintenance, replacement frequency, durability, and energy usage. The life cycle is the useful life for a building prior to a major rehabilitation or removal, usually forty years for a commercial building but shorter for hospitals, processing plants, and research laboratories. Different components have different lives, masonry walls being relatively long and some air conditioning components being relatively short.

Liquidated Damages: Losses incurred by the owner (almost always in the public sector) due to a project duration extending beyond a contractual completion date. These losses (damages) are usually projected as costs per day and are liquidated by withholding payments from the contractor. The terms of liquidated damages must be established in the contract document so that bidders can consider them in estimating a project. To be fully legally binding, liquidated damages should be rationally related to actual losses incurred by owner.

Long-Lead Procurement; Long-Lead-Time Item: A building component that requires long design and fabrication period and thus should be ordered early to the owner, contractor, or construction manager. The item then is typically assigned to the contractor for installation.

Lump Sum: A fixed price for an agreement upon project or amount of work; a project delivery system based on an agreement whereby the contractor or subcontractor performs a specific scope of work for a fixed cost agreement upon prior to commencement of construction and altered only by changes in the work agreed upon by both parties.

Manufacturer's Representative: An employee or private operative who provides information to owners, designers, and constructors on materials and equipment.

Mark-Up: Amount, usually overhead and profit, that the contractor adds to direct cost prior to billing the owner; likewise used by subcontractors in billing contractors.

Master Builder: Part fact and part myth, the individual, usually a master stonemason who organized and led the design and construction of medieval buildings.

Material; Material Costs: The segment of the work represented by building materials, temporary materials and certain equipment.

Minority Business Enterprise (MBE): A business that is wholly or partly owned by persons declared to be minorities by legislation, usually African Americans, Native Americans, and certain other ethnic groups. Many governmental units require some level of MBE involvement in construction contracts.

Modularization: Factory-made or other off-site assembly of units for installation during construction; also referred to as componentization.

National Society of Professional Engineers: A national association, many members of which provide services for building design and construction. NSPE promotes education, principles and standards of practice, and professional advice to members.

Negligence: Failure of one party to protect the health or interest of another party property; failure to practice a prudent degree of care.

Notice: Any one of several official written communications from one party authorizing or requiring another party to act or to cease acting:

> **Notice to Bidders:** Owner or architect provides information or requests proposals from those so notified.

> **Notice of Change:** A communication from the owner or architect to the contractor to announce a change in the work covered by a contract and indented to initiate the necessary negotiations to reach agreement on the change.

> **Notice to Proceed:** Owner authorizes the contractor to begin work on a project on a particular day or "as soon as possible," such notice is linked to the duration of a project.

Observation of the Work: Part of a designer's activity during construction, related to contract administration, with the objective of assuming that the work is proceeding according to contract documents; less than supervision, with no responsibility for means or methods.

Occupancy: Classification of use of a building, primarily for building code purposes, as different occupancies require responsibility for means or methods.

Open Bidding: Vernacular term for bidding process without pre-qualification or restriction.

OSHA: Occupational Safety and Health Administration, an agency with the U.S. Department of Labor that is empowered by legislation to promulgate standards, rules, and regulations on safety and health in industry. Most states have their own safety agencies that generally duplicate the national system.

Overhead: Project costs not directly related to labor, material, and equipment:

> **Job Overhead:** Includes those costs that can be accurately allocated to a particular project, such as job office secretary, utilities, phone, and security.

> **Office Overhead:** Includes those activities in the home office that cannot be allocated to particular jobs and that must be covered to varying degrees by all the projects of a company.

Owner: The party to the contract who has legal possession of the property or who is duly selected to represent the property owner, and who typically provides the financing for the construction. The owner may or may not be the primary user of the property. In the case of a public school, the owners are the taxpayers of the district represented by the board of education, and the users are the teachers and students.

Partnering: A formal structure to establish a working relationship among all the stakeholders through a mutually developed strategy of commitment and communication. There are two principal partnering variations.

> **Individual Project Partnering:** The owner, key contractors, and designers agree to cooperate on quality

standards, information exchanges, and dispute avoidance. The process does not follow a standard form but usually involves a pre-construction conference, set of agreements, and charger of cooperation signed by all parties.

Long Term Relationship Partnering: A relationship between the owner and the construction company or design firm wherein the owner agrees to award a series of contracts to the construction company in return for assurances of priority service. These are sometimes called alliance agreements or preferred supplier agreements.

Partnership: Business or professional organization in which two or more persons agree in writing to merge their talents and assets to create an entity that is identified with all the partners. The partners become liable for each other's business obligations and can be at risk for losses incurred by individual partners.

Penalty Clause: A contractual inclusion (different from liquidated damages) that reduces the contract sum based on inadequate performance on the part of the contractor usually tied to project duration. May be offset by an incentive clause.

Per Diem: Literally means "per day," related to the cost of services or reimbursement based on the number of days (or parts thereof) that a person is retained. For many professional services, it is more typical to charge per hour.

Phased Construction: A process involving the construction of one or more buildings over a period of time with different start dates and completion dates, usually involving owner's sequential occupancy needs over time. This term also relates to a series of bid packages wherein different trade contractors perform different parts of the project through phases; somewhat analogous to fast tracking.

Post-Construction Services: A range of activities performed following the actual construction process, including commissioning, start-up, warranty documentation, and maintenance.

Pre-Construction Services: A range of activities performed by a contractor prior to execution of construction, including value engineering, constructability, cost and schedule studies, procurement of long lead time items, and staffing requirements.

Prefabrication; Pre-Assembly: Fabrication external to the building envelope (on-site or off-site to reduce labor costs, reduce congestion, and compress schedule).

Pre-Qualification: Sometimes simply called qualification, a process for determining whether a contractor has the ability, credentials, financial strength, and personnel to carry out a project. Formal pre-qualification employs standard forms such as those by AIA or AGC and includes statements of experience, key personnel, and audited financial records.

Prime Contract: Agreement between an owner and prime contractor, usually using a standard form available such as AIA or AGC, which spells out the obligations of the parties, including work to be done, approval process, payment, and conditions of the contract.

Prime Contractor: The person or company who has an agreement directly with the owner. Usually these are general contractors but may be mechanical or other trade or specialty contractors who sign direct agreements with owners because of either state laws or the owners' requirement, such as in agency construction management.

Private Work: Projects that have no public funding. Compared to public work, statutory requirements are much less rigorous in private work, with agreements typically being controlled by commercial codes and statutes of fraud. There are many opportunities for innovation in delivery systems, cost savings, schedule compression, and negotiations on a variety of issues.

Private/Public Work Projects: Projects that have components that are publicly funded and components that are privately financed. Examples are inner city projects where municipalities build site improvements such as utilities, access ramps, streets, sidewalks, and parking garages and then provide building sites (sometimes air rights) for private development.

Procurement: The process of buying and obtaining the necessary property, design, contracts, labor, materials, and equipment to build a project. In the context of construction projects, procurement refers to the general contractor buying the subcontracts, labor, and materials.

Production: Output over time; units completed per week or month; useful for measuring schedule compliance but not for measuring cost efficiency.

Productivity: Comparison of output to input; that is, value of billable work compared to costs of labor, material, and overhead; the rate of production compared to benchmarks; a part of overall project strategy; a key element of profitability.

Profit: The amount of money remaining after all expenses on a project have been paid, including both job and office overhead; the amount on which company income taxes must be paid. Uses of profit include building up reserves, investment in new equipment, training, and bonuses to employees and dividends to stockholders if the company is a corporation.

Profitability: A measure of net return or potential net return on investment, including investment in construction by either owner or contractor.

Program: See under "design."

Program Management: A project delivery "set of processes" based on an agreement whereby a construction entity provides comprehensive agency services to an owner from the programming stage through occupancy. The p.m.essentially becomes a surrogate owner, providing all the procurement and coordination of design, construction, closeout and move in, but does not take on the contractual liability for design of construction.

Project: The physical and contractual definition of the execution of construction of one or more buildings; the total work being done. Related items:

> **Project Agreement:** A set of agreed-upon conditions between labor and management on a particular project, typically including labor representation, wage rates, hiring practices, strike avoidance provisions, and dispute resolution processes. Project agreements may be used in union setting as alternatives to periodic collective bargaining agreements.

> **Project Costing:** See "costing."

> **Project Executive:** An elevated project manager, one in charge of several projects; or simply the name used by some companies for project managers.

Project Manager: One who is responsible overall for a project, particularly awarding subcontracts, procuring materials, monitoring costs, and managing the paperwork; usually office based.

Project Manual: Written parts of the contract documents including specifications, conditions, forms of agreement, and forms of proposal, bound together; sometimes refers to a contractor's binder of many guidance documents and instructions.

Project Preplanning: A formal process of identifying many aspects of a project that need early decisions and assigning those decisions to a particular person; developing a strategy for project execution and ideally placing all of the resulting documents into a construction project manual.

Project Superintendant: See "superintendant."

Project Delivery System: A comprehensive process wherein designers, constructors, and various consultants provide services for design and construction to deliver a built project to the owner.

Property: Identifiable assets of owned interest; may be "real" as in land and buildings; "personal," which are typically portable; or "intangible," which are various forms of paper interests such as stocks and bonds.

Proposal: An offer to perform services or work, usually including a price and other stipulations such as time, level of performance, and description of the end product. The term is somewhat interchangeable with "bid," except that a bid is based on specific conditions and a proposal may be either general or specific.

Proprietorship: An individually owned business wherein one person takes all the risks and keeps all the profits or absorbs all the losses. New construction entities are frequently proprietorships because there is little cost or legal requirement to become a proprietor. However, licenses are required in many states to perform construction. Once successful, proprietorships frequently become corporations.

Public Work: Projects that are paid for totally or in part by public funds; i.e., taxpayers' dollars, whether at the national, state, or local level. Public work carries statutory requirements for advertisement, bidding, contractor selection, and bonding. Other considerations such as prevailing wage, minority business involvement, and liquidated damages are required by various governmental units for certain contracts.

Publicly Guaranteed Private Work: Projects that are privately owned and operated but carry governmental backing either by guaranteeing private financing or issuing special bonds. Such projects are those that are in the public interest but function best under private ownership. They usually are not profitable ventures. These include hospitals, special housing, and business enterprises of particular value to local communities. These projects are usually contracted much like public work, with all the legal requirements.

Punch List; Item List: A schedule of work remaining to be done to complete a project, usually the result of a "walk through" by the parties at the time of substantial completion and enumerating the activities to be performed to reach final completion. The punch list should be agreed upon by the owner, designer, and contractor and should not there after be altered unless a product failure occurs during the punch-out period.

Quality, Quality Control: Pertaining to the many efforts both formal and informal by designers and constructors to select products and to monitor the execution of construction to assure a high level of quality of the resulting building.

Quantity Surveying: Accounting for all the materials in a project, an early step in estimating process. In the British Commonwealth, quantity surveying is a professional that provides bidders with a list of materials.

Quotation: The monetary or price aspects of a bid or proposal to perform work or a service.

Record Drawings: A marked-up set of drawings showing any changes that took place during construction. Sometimes called as-build drawings. In CAD systems, they may be on a disk.

Reimbursable: Those costs that are expanded by consultants or contractors and are directly reimbursed by owners, perhaps with a small multiple, including printing, travel, and special purchases. In const-plus, a fee contracts labor and materials.

Retainage (Retention): The practice of holding back part of periodic payments to contractors, aimed at avoiding the risk to the owner of paying ore than the actual built value and to assure an adequate pool of funds in case of default by the contractor. Sureties are particularly supportive of retainage. There are many variations, but typical contract provisions are for 10 percent retainage on payments making up the first 50 percent of the contract amount, which then becomes 5 percent held back on substantial completion. Prime contractors routinely retain similar percentages from subcontractors. All retained amounts should be placed in escrow and should be paid at the time of final completion, with interest, if the agreement so stipulates.

Risk: The concept or act of exposing oneself or one's company to possible loss, usually while engaging in an enterprise for profit.

Samples: Representative examples of products or materials to be used in buildings, submitted by the contractor to the architect or owner for approval prior to actual installation. Samples range from bricks to finished woodwork.

Schedule: An organized array of information to illustrate resource allocation, interrelationships of activities, costs, and performances. There are many types of schedules and scheduling terms related to construction. The following are adapted from the AGC Publication Construction Planning and Scheduling, by Thomas Glavinich and Paul Stella:

> **Activity Logic:** Relationships determine the sequence that activities can or will be carried out during construction based on physical safety, resource, and preferential relationship considerations.

> **As-Build Schedule:** Historical record of a project in the form of a schedule showing actual activity start and finish dates.

> **As-Planned Schedule:** The way in which the project is planned to be completed in the form of a schedule showing planned activity start and finish dates.

> **Bar Chart:** Graphic representation of a project that includes the activities that make up the project, the estimated duration of each activity, and the planned sequence of activity performance. Activities are represented by bars placed on the schedule with a time

line along the horizontal axis and a list of activities along the vertical axis.

Cost Loading: Assigning the estimated activity cost to activities in a schedule.

Critical Path: Longest continuous chain of activities through the network schedule that establishes the minimum overall project duration.

Early Finish: The earliest an activity can finish given that activity's early start and duration.

Early Start: The earliest an activity can start after all predecessors to the activity are completed.

Gantt Chart: Another name for a bar chart, named for Henry L. Gantt, who developed the bar chart.

Late Finish: The latest that an activity can finish and still complete the project within the minimum overall duration determined by the forward pass.

Late Start: The latest that an activity can start and still complete the project within the minimum overall duration.

Look-Ahead Schedule: The focus on a short period of time and what needs to be accomplished on the project within the context of the overall project schedule. Look-ahead schedules typically deal with activities that need to be started, worked on, or finished within the following week(s) or month.

Milestones: Important dates included in schedules for reference or measurement. Milestones do not consume any time or resource. An example of a milestone is "building enclosed."

Network Scheduling: Method of planning and scheduling a construction project where activities are arranged based on activity relationships and network calculations, which determine when activities can be performed and the critical path of the project.

Resource Leveling: Attempts to keep the demand for a particular resource as constant as possible during the period that the resource is needed.

Schedule Compression: Reduction of the overall project duration through changes in activity logic or the reduction of activity durations.

Schedule Update: Revision of the project schedule to reflect the current status of activities at the time of the update as well as how the project is planned to be completed.

Schedule of Values: A breakdown of a contract sum into activity costs to serve as a basis of progress payments by the owner to the contractor. The schedule of values interrelated to the time schedule determines the amount of each progress payment.

Schematic: See "design."

Scope of Work: A contractual term describing the overall boundaries of work included in a contract, such as site and building geometry, extent of improvements, and particular equipment.

Selection; Selection Process: Procedure in making an important decision, particularly as it relates to choosing designers or contractors.

Self-Performance: Work done directly by a prime contractor. This may be covered in the prime contract (some states have laws regarding self-performance) or it may be left to the contractors. An important project pre-planning decision is the amount of self-performance vs. subcontracting to be done on a project.

Services: A broad term with a number of meanings, those most frequently used in construction being the valued activities provided to owners by designers and constructors, and utility services such as water, sewers, electric, gas, and phone.

Shop Drawings: Detailed graphics of equipment or building components prepared by manufacturers, vendors, or subcontractors of the items. The drawings are used for production, fabrication, and installation of the components and are necessarily approved by both designers and contractors prior to execution of that segment of the work.

Site: The location of the project, usually defined by surveyed meters and bounds, or construction limit boundaries.

Specifications: See "contract documents."

Standard; Standards: A general term used to identify levels of expected performance of frequently used items and services, such as standards of professional practice, standard forms of agreement, and standard equipment.

Stipulated Sum: Lump sum or fixed price.

Subcontract: Agreement between contractor and subcontractor usually using a standard form available from AIA, AGC, or other associations. The owner is typically not a party to a subcontract, thus the obligations between the owner and the subcontractor must flow through the prime contractor.

Substantial Completion: A condition in which the owner can take partial or full occupancy of a project despite some work still needing to be done (such work being enumerated on a punch list). A certificate of occupancy is required from the building authority for the owner to take occupancy. Usually the remaining contractual amount is paid to the contractor at this time except for any accumulated retainage. In the absence of retainage, an amount estimated to equal the value of the punch list is withheld.

Superintendent: Contractor's job site supervisor, charged with coordinating and directing operations toward the completion of the project.

Supervisor: Any person charged with directing the work of others, such as a foreman or superintendent.

Supplier: A company or person who provides materials, equipment, or components to a project. Sometimes the supplier is under direct contract with the contractor, sometimes not. The term *vendor* can be used.

Surety: See "bonds."

Take-Off: Vernacular term for quantity survey.

Target Price: A cost goal; non-exact projected cost of construction; budgeted cost; may become a guaranteed maximum price.

Tender: A bid or proposed price.

Third Party: One who is not a party to the contract but who interacts with one or more of the contractual parties in some way. Examples include inspectors, testing agencies, and underwriters.

Tort: A civil action or suit that is based on the belief that one party wronged another party. Workplace tort or employer tort refers to an action by an employee against an employer for perceived negligence that damaged the employee.

Trade Contractor: See "contractor."

Tradesperson: One who practices mechanical skills in construction, such as a carpenter, mason, or roofer; also called craftsperson.

Turnkey: A type of project delivery system within the category of design-build in which the contractor provides financing, design, and construction under a performance set of specifications and provides a completed project for an agreed-upon price. Upon completion, the contractor turns the key over to the owner in return for full payment.

Underwriter: One who guarantees or insures the work or debts of another; a provider of insurance contracts.

Unit Price: Bid cost (priced in advance) for anticipated extra work, such as additional excavation or concrete. Highway construction is sometimes bid totally with unit prices.

Upset Price: A vernacular term for a contractual clause describing the division of savings on the project with a guaranteed maximum price. The contractor may be entitled to a percentage of the cost savings as incentive.

Utility: A publicly distributed service such as electric, water, phone, and gas.

Value Engineering: A design process involving critical evaluation of elements of a building to determine the relative value to the owner of the specified product or system compared to alternative products or systems. Life-cycle costing and constructability studies may be pats of value engineering processes.

Waiver of Lien: See "lien."

Warranty: A statement supplied by a manufacturer, supplier, or contractor for material, equipment, or components that provide replacement or reimbursement, usually on a basis of diminishing value over time, in case of faulty performance or failure of a product. Two common types of warranties are:

> **Express Warranty:** A written statement specifying the terms related to the product.

> **Implied Warranty:** Usually covered by uniform commercial codes that specify that any product sold in a bona fide sale shall be merchantable and free of known defects.

Women's Business Enterprise (WBE): A business that is wholly or partially owned by a woman. In some governmental units, construction contracts are required to have certain percentages of WBE.

Work: The labor required to produce a built project, the project itself, or a branch of construction as in public work.

Workers' Compensation: See "insurance."

Working Drawings: Detailed drawings used for construction; a principal component of contract documents.

Wrap-Up Policy: See "insurance."

Wrecking: Related to construction in that many sites must be cleared of other structures before construction can begin; a branch of construction involving the removal of buildings or components and requiring a permit in most jurisdictions.

Yard: Place or facility where a contractor stores or maintains equipment and materials. In zoning, the space required between a property line and a building.

Zoning Regulations: Employed in practically all urban areas, many counties and some states regulate land use based on the police power to protect the health, safety, and welfare of citizens and manifested by restrictions on types of land use (industrial, commercial, residential, etc.) degree of site coverage, heights, and setbacks.